THE WESTCOASTER
COOKBOOK – VOLUME II

SEAFOOD

Jean & Phil Hood
Dawn Bolton

Maple Lane Publishing

Dedicated to the Great Fisherman
Who dwells within.

© 1995 Maple Lane Mediaworks Inc.
All Rights Reserved

First Printing 1995
1996 (revised), 1997, 1998, 2000 (revised)
Sixth Printing 2002 (complete revision)

ISBN No. 0-921966-12-1

Cover Design & Pre-Press Production by Phil Hood, Mediaworks Inc.
British Columbia, Canada

"Fisherman Cat" by Marcia Perrin
Photography by Phil Hood and John Chinnery

Printed in Canada

Maple Lane Publishing
Toll-Free Order Number
1-800-270-6007
      www.the-westcoaster.com

Contents

A Westcoast fishermen's seafood cookbook down-to-earth, practical, yet full of surprises!

What do you do when you have a cardboard box overflowing with seafood recipes? You publish a seafood cookbook called "The Westcoaster Seafood Cookbook," of course—or at least this is what Jean and Phil Hood and their friend Dawn Bolton have done.

Jean and Phil have roots that go back to the Village of Ucluelet, located on the West Coast of Vancouver Island. Dawn is from the Washington seacoast community of Edmonds.

"I used to brag that Jean had 100 different ways to cook salmon," says Phil.

Their love affair with west coast seafood cooking began one summer when Phil worked on a Ucluelet fuel dock. "I served commercial fishermen and often received fresh seafood as a tip. Our freezer quickly filled up with salmon, cod, halibut, shrimp or almost any type of eatable seafood from the ocean. We soon bored of ordinary stand-by seafood recipes. Jean called all her west coast friends and started what became a huge collection of seafood specialties."

Today, Phil and his son Richard (the cute kid on the cover, now grown-up), are the primary seafood cooks of the family. "Our barbecue salmon is great, but after poached, baked and smoked salmon—battered deep-fried red snapper has to be a family favorite. Our most famous specialty is "smoked salmon cheese cake spread" and our most fun recipe is a tomato-based Cioppino (soup) that we call our BYOF party soup."

"I think cooking our catch is as much fun as catching it in the first place," says Phil. "But we really don't have any hang-ups about using market, frozen or canned seafood."

The "Westcoaster" name comes from a community newspaper that Jean and Phil owned and published for eight years in the Ucluelet-Tofino area.

Batters, Stuffings, Sauces, Marinades, Dips & More

This section of the Westcoaster Seafood Cookbook deals with the inside and the outside of the fish. Delicious batters for deep frying and tantalizing stuffings to compliment the flavor of the fish.

How do you turn a plainly cooked piece of fish into a gourmet dinner? Dip it in a spicy dip. Dress it up with a colorful sauce. Marinate it in a delectable marinade. Or try the Westcoaster Shakin' Bake mix on page 114! Choose one of our delicious recipes and go for it!

Basic Fish Batter

Ingredients:
- 1 ½ cups (375 ml) prepared pancake **mix**
- 1 ½ cups (375 ml) **milk**
- ¾ tsp (4 ml) **salt**
- Flour

Method:
In a large bowl combine first three ingredients until well blended. See directions for deep frying fish, this page under Ucluelet Crispy Beer Batter.

Ucluelet Crispy Beer Batter

Ingredients:
- 1 ½ cups (375 ml) all-purpose **flour**
- ¾ tsp (4 ml) **salt**
- 1 cup (250 ml) **beer**
- ¼ cup (60 ml) vegetable **oil**
- 3 **egg whites**
- Flour
- Oil

Method:
In a medium-size bowl, combine flour and salt, mix in beer and oil. Let stand in a warm place for 20-30 minutes. Beat egg whites until stiff and gently fold into flour mixture. Cut fish into uniform sizes. Rinse fish, pat dry, dip into flour, then into batter, let excess batter drip off. In a deep-fryer or deep heavy pan, gently drop fish in hot oil (375°F/190°C) and fry fish until golden brown and crispy. Always fry in small batches. The fish should be opaque and flake when tested with a fork, about 5-7 minutes. Batter should be golden. Enough to coat 2 cups (500 ml) of fish.

Deep Frying Batter for Fish

Ingredients:
- 1 cup (250 ml) sifted all-purpose **flour**
- 1 tsp (5 ml) **baking powder**
- 2 **eggs**, beaten
- 1 cup (250 ml) **water**
- 1 Tbsp (15 ml) **vinegar**

Method:
Combine flour and baking powder together in a large bowl. Add eggs and water; beat well. Add vinegar and beat again. Do not add salt to this recipe as it will ruin the batter. See directions for deep frying fish on page 6 (under Ucluelet Crispy Beer Batter).

West Coast Salmon Stuffing

Contributed by Gladys Lancaster, Abbotsford, B.C., Canada

Ingredients:
- 5 strips **bacon**, chopped
- 1 lb (454 g) fresh **mushrooms**, chopped
- 2 stalks **celery**, chopped
- 1 large **onion**, diced
- 2 cups (500 ml) cooked **brown rice**
- 1 Tbsp (15 ml) **parsley**, chopped
- ½ tsp (2 ml) **dill seeds**

Method:
In saucepan, fry bacon slightly. Stir in rest of ingredients and cook for five minutes. This is enough stuffing for a whole salmon. See Salmon Guidelines for baking fish on page 72.

Vancouver Clam Stuffing

Ingredients:
- ½ cup (125 ml) **clams**, chopped
- 2 cups (500 ml) **cracker crumbs**, crushed fine
- 2 Tbsp (30 ml) **butter** OR **margarine**, melted
- **Salt** and **pepper** to taste
- 2 tsp (10 ml) **pickle**, chopped
- 2 Tbsp (30 ml) **lemon juice**
- ½ cup (125 ml) **water** OR ¼ cup (60 ml) **water** and ¼ cup (60 ml) **clam liquor**

Method:

In a large bowl, mix together all ingredients in the order given. If you prefer a more moist dressing, add more water. Makes enough to stuff a 3-4 lb (1.5-2 kg) fish. See Salmon Guidelines for baking fish on page 72.

Mushroom Stuffing

Ingredients:
- ¼ cup (60 ml) **butter** OR **margarine**
- ¼ cup (60 ml) **celery**, minced
- ¼ cup (60 ml) **onion**, minced
- ¼-½ lb (125-225 g) **mushrooms**, sliced
- 1 Tbsp (15 ml) **parsley**, minced
- 2 cups (500 ml) **crackers**, coarsely crushed
- ¼ tsp (1 ml) poultry **seasoning**
- **Salt** to taste

Method:

Melt butter or margarine in a large skillet. Sauté celery and onion. When onion is a golden brown add mushrooms and cook for 3 minutes. Add remaining ingredients and mix well. This makes enough for a 4-6 lb (2-3 kg) fish. Recipe may be halved for smaller fish. This stuffing is also excellent rolled up in fillets and baked. See Salmon Guidelines for baking fish on page 72.

8

Vegetable Stuffing

Ingredients:
  2 medium-size **carrots**,
  coarsely shredded
  ¼ cup (60 ml) **celery**, finely
  chopped
  3 Tbsp (45 ml) **parsley**,
  chopped

Method:
  In a small bowl, combine all
ingredients. Loosely stuff fish.
This is a nice change from the
traditional cracker or bread
stuffing. See Salmon Guidelines
for baking fish on page 72.

Rice Stuffing with Lemon

Ingredients:
  6 Tbsp (90 ml) **butter** OR
  margarine, divided
  1 cup (250 ml) **celery**,
  sliced
  1 small **onion**, chopped
  ¼ tsp (1 ml) **thyme**
  2 tsp (10 ml) **lemon peel**,
  grated
  ¼ cup (60 ml) **lemon juice**
  2 ½ cups (625 ml) **water**
  1 ¼ cups (310 ml)
  long-grain white **rice**
  1 ½ cups (375 ml)
  mushrooms, sliced
  Salt and **pepper** to taste

Method:
  Melt 3 Tbsp (45 ml) butter in
large saucepan. Sauté celery
and onion, stirring until just
soft, about 5 minutes. Add to
the sautéed celery and onion
the thyme, lemon peel, lemon
juice and water. Bring to a
boil. Stir in the rice and cover.
Reduce heat to a low simmer
and cook for 20 minutes or
until all liquid is absorbed.

  While rice is cooking melt
remaining butter in a skillet.
Sauté mushrooms until soft.
Stir sautéed mushrooms, salt
and pepper into rice. Makes
enough to stuff an 8 lb (3.5 kg)
fish. Excellent with salmon.
See Salmon Guidelines
for baking fish on
page 72.

9

Sweet Tomato-Chili Sauce

Ingredients:
- 2 Tbsp (30 ml) salad **oil**
- 4 fresh mild green **chilies**, stems and seeds removed and chopped
- 2 medium **onions**, chopped
- 1 **garlic clove**, minced
- 8 medium sized **tomatoes** peeled, seeded and diced
- 1 ½ cups (375 ml) cider **vinegar**
- 1 ½ cups (375 ml) **sugar**
- 2 ½ tsp (12 ml) **salt**
- 1 tsp (5 ml) **Worcestershire sauce**

Method:

In a heavy 4 qt (4 l) saucepan over medium heat, heat oil and cook chilies, onions, and garlic until tender. Stir in tomatoes, vinegar, sugar, salt and Worcestershire sauce. Over high heat, heat to boiling. Reduce heat to medium and simmer uncovered, until mixture thickens and is reduced to about 3 cups (750 ml) about 1 ½ hours. Stir often.

Mushroom Sauce

Contributed by Wanda Brown, Delta, B.C., Canada
Try with Baked Salmon!

Ingredients:
- 2 Tbsp (30 ml) **butter**
- 1 small **onion**, chopped
- 1 lb (454 g) **mushrooms**, cleaned and sliced
- 1 tub (10 oz/284 ml) dairy **sour cream**
- 1 tsp (5 ml) **dill weed**
- ½ tsp (2 ml) **garlic powder**
- **Salt** and **pepper** to taste

Method:

Heat butter in a large skillet. Add onion and cook until transparent. Add mushrooms and continue cooking until all are just browned. Stir in sour cream and seasonings, stirring until smooth. Cover and cook over low heat until heated through. Do not boil. If sauce seems too thin you may add 1 Tbsp (15 ml) flour to thicken.

Mustard Sauce

Mustard Sauce is delicious with any fried seafood!

Ingredients:
- ½ cup (125 ml) **mayonnaise**
- 1 Tbsp (15 ml) Dijon-style **mustard**
- 1 Tbsp (15 ml) Red wine **vinegar**
- ½ tsp (2 ml) **sugar** (optional)
- **Salt** and **pepper** to taste

Method:

Combine all ingredients in a small glass bowl. Refrigerate until ready to use.

Cocktail Sauce

Great with shrimp!

Ingredients:
- 3 Tbsp (45 ml) **mayonnaise**
- ½ cup (125 ml) **chili sauce**
- Juice of 1 **lemon**
- 1 Tbsp (15 ml) Dijon-style **mustard**
- 1 Tbsp (15 ml) prepared **horseradish**

Method:

Combine all ingredients in a small bowl. Chill for 1 hour to blend flavors.

Lemon Sauce

Ingredients:
- ¼ cup (60 ml) **soy sauce**
- 1 Tbsp (15 ml) **lemon juice**

Method:

Combine ingredients in a small glass bowl. Sauce may be heated or served cold.

Remoulade Sauce

Fantastic with shellfish!

Ingredients:
- 2 **eggs**, hard-cooked
- 1 tsp (5 ml) **lemon juice**
- ¾ cup (175 ml) light **mayonnaise**
- 1 tsp (5 ml) sour **gherkins**, minced
- 1 tsp (5 ml) Dijon-style **mustard**
- **Salt** and **pepper** to taste
- 1 tsp (5 ml) **chives**
- 1 tsp (5 ml) **tarragon**
- 1 tsp (5 ml) **capers**

Method:

Remove yolks from hard-cooked eggs. In a small bowl mash egg yolks with lemon juice until a smooth paste is formed. Add mayonnaise, gherkins, mustard, salt and pepper to yolk mixture and blend well. Stir in chives, tarragon and capers, cover. Keep refrigerated until served.

Tartar Sauce

Delicious with fish & chips, burgers and fish cakes!

Ingredients:
- ½ cup (125 ml) **mayonnaise**
- 1 **clove garlic**, minced or pressed
- 1 tsp (5 ml) **capers**, chopped (optional)
- 1 Tbsp (15 ml) **parsley**, chopped fine
- 2 sweet **gherkins**, chopped fine OR 1 Tbsp (15 ml) green **relish**

Method:

In a small glass bowl, mix together all ingredients, cover and chill for 1 hour.

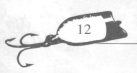

Heather's Raspberry Salsa

Try this with baked salmon for a special treat!

Ingredients:
- 2 cups (500 ml) **raspberries**, fresh or frozen
- 2 **peaches**, peeled, fresh or canned, chopped fine
- ½ Long English **cucumber**, chopped fine
- ¼ cup (60 ml) **onions**, diced
- 2 Tbsp (30 ml) fresh **parsley**, chopped fine
- 2 Tbsp (30 ml) **cilantro** leaves, chopped fine
- **Salt** to taste
- **Sugar** to taste (optional)

Method:

Combine all ingredients in a glass bowl, mix well, cover and refrigerate for at least 2 hours.

Oriental Basting Marinade

This is especially good on halibut!

Ingredients:
- ¼ cup (60 ml) **orange juice**
- 2 Tbsp (30 ml) **soy sauce**
- 2 Tbsp (30 ml) **catsup**
- 2 Tbsp (30 ml) **parsley**, chopped
- 2 Tbsp (30 ml) salad **oil**
- 1 Tbsp (15 ml) **lemon juice**
- ½ tsp (2 ml) **oregano**
- ½ tsp (2 ml) **pepper**
- 1 **clove garlic**, minced

Method:

Combine ingredients in a small glass or stainless steel bowl. Cover and refrigerate for 1 hour to blend flavors. Brush fish during cooking. Makes ¾ cup (175 ml).

Jim's Barbecue Sauce for Salmon

Contributed by Jim Lundberg, Abbotsford, B.C., Canada

Ingredients:
- 4 **cloves garlic**, crushed
- ¼ cup (60 ml) **butter**
- 1 cup (250 ml) **lemon juice**
- 1 ½ Tbsp (22 ml) **brown sugar**
- 1 tsp (5 ml) **corn starch**

Method:
In a small saucepan, sauté garlic over low heat in melted butter for 5 minutes. Add lemon juice and sugar, stir. Simmer for 5 more minutes, stirring occasionally. Mix in corn starch until smooth. Stir over moderate heat to thicken. Take off heat and brush on fish as you barbecue.

Smoky Marinade & Barbecue Sauce

Ingredients:
- ¼ cup (60 ml) **olive oil**
- ½ cup (125 ml) **chili sauce**
- ¼ cup (60 ml) **vinegar**
- 1 ½ tsp (7 ml) **Worcestershire sauce**
- 2 Tbsp (30 ml) hickory-flavored **liquid smoke**
- 1 ½ tsp (7 ml) **onion**, chopped
- ½ **clove garlic**, minced
- **Salt** to taste
- 2 Tbsp (30 ml) **brown sugar**

Method:
In a small glass or stainless steel bowl blend all ingredients together. Place fish in large glass dish. Pour marinade over fish, cover and refrigerate for about 1 hour, preferably 2 hours. Turn occasionally. Use sauce for basting fish while cooking.

Tim's B-B-Q Salmon Marinade

Contributed by Teresa Bird, Port McNeill, B.C., Canada

Ingredients:
Water
2 cups (500 ml) cider
  vinegar
2 cups (500 ml) **brown
  sugar**

Method:
In a large glass or stainless steel mixing bowl, pour in water until half full. Add cider vinegar and brown sugar. Stir until sugar dissolved. Add fish, cover and refrigerate. Marinate for at least 12 hours, turning fish occasionally. Drain, place fish on foil, skin side down and barbecue according to recipe.

West Coast Marinade

Ingredients:
½ cup (125 ml) **olive oil**
1 **clove garlic**, minced
½ tsp (2 ml) black **pepper**
½ tsp (2 ml) **oregano**
½ cup (125 ml) **lemon
  juice**
½ tsp (2 ml) **salt**
½ tsp (2 ml) **parsley**,
  minced

Method:
Combine ingredients in a shallow glass dish. Add fish, cover and refrigerate for at least 1 hour. Turn fish occasionally. Use marinade to baste fish during cooking.

15

Teriyaki Marinade

Ingredients:
- ½ cup (125 ml) **soy sauce**
- 2 heaping Tbsp (30 ml) **honey**
- 3 Tbsp (45 ml) **sugar** (white OR brown)
- 1 tsp (5 ml) **Accent** (optional)
- 1 tsp (5 ml) **Mirin**
- 2 **clove**s of **garlic**, chopped fine
- Scant ½ tsp (2 ml) fresh **ginger**, peeled and grated
- 1 small **onion**, sliced (optional)

Method:
In a small glass bowl, mix all ingredients well. Place fish in large glass or stainless steel dish. Pour marinade over fish, cover, refrigerate and let stand about 1 hour, turning fish at least once. When ready to use, drain fish, pat dry if frying and use according to recipe.

Ginger-Pineapple Marinade

Ingredients:
- ¼ cup (60 ml) **pineapple juice**
- 2 Tbsp (30 ml) **rice wine vinegar**
- 1 tsp (5 ml) **soy sauce**
- 2 tsp (10 ml) vegetable OR olive **oil**
- 1 tsp (5 ml) fresh **ginger**, peeled and grated
- 1 tsp (5 ml) **garlic**, minced

Method:
In a small glass bowl, mix all ingredients well. Pour over fish in a shallow glass dish and cover. Refrigerate for at least 1 hour, turning frequently.

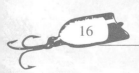

SEAFOOD

Raspberry Salsa 13

Kiwanda
Salmon Fritters 108

Checleset Bay
Salmon Balls 102

Salmon Swirls with
Cheese Sauce 109

Deep Frying Batter for Fish 7

Tartar
Sauce 12

Cajun Marinade

Ingredients:
- ½ cup (125 ml) **olive oil**
- ¼ cup (60 ml) **vinegar**
- ½ tsp (2 ml) fresh ground black **pepper**
- ½ tsp (2 ml) **dry mustard**
- ½ tsp (2 ml) hot **pepper** flakes
- 1 tsp (5 ml) **brown sugar**
- 1 tsp (5 ml) **thyme**
- 1 tsp (5 ml) **oregano**
- 1 tsp (5 ml) sweet OR hot **paprika**
- 1 tsp (5 ml) coarse **salt**

Method:

Combine all ingredients in a small glass bowl, mix well. For every pound (500 g) of fish, marinate with about ⅓ cup (80 ml) of marinade. Cover and refrigerate for 30 minutes, turning occasionally.

Mediterranean Spice Rub

Ingredients:
- 3 Tbsp (45 ml) dried **rosemary**
- 2 Tbsp (30 ml) dried **parsley**
- 2 Tbsp (30 ml) dried **dill**
- 3 Tbsp (45 ml) dried **basil**
- 1 Tbsp (15 ml) dried **oregano**
- ½ tsp (2 ml) fresh ground black **pepper corns**
- ½ tsp (2 ml) dry **mustard**
- ½ tsp (2 ml) hot **pepper** flakes
- 1 tsp (5 ml) coarse **salt**
- 1 tsp (5 ml) **garlic powder**

Method:

Combine ingredients in a glass bowl, mix well. For every pound (500 g) of fish, rub 2 Tbsp (30 ml) mixture, with your fingers gently onto the fish, cover and refrigerate for at least 4-12 hours, turning occasionally. Or, combine 4 tsp (20 ml) of mixture with 1 Tbsp (15 ml) olive oil, brush on fish, cover and refrigerate for 15 minutes up to 4 hours, turning occasionally. Discard any rub that came into contact with raw fish once you are finished. Store remainder of dry rub in an air-tight container. Keeps up to 6 months.

Marinade for Smoked Salmon

Contributed by Sharon Johnson, Esperanza, B.C., Canada

Ingredients:
Equal parts **soy sauce** and **brown sugar**

Method:
In a glass, stainless steel or food-grade plastic, combine soy sauce and brown sugar. Marinade fish in this mixture overnight. Smoke 1 to 2 days depending on desired moistness.

Dave Crampton's Salmon Brine

Contributed by Jeanette Cazzola, Sidney, B.C., Canada

Ingredients:
⅓ cup (80 ml) **white sugar**
¼ cup (60 ml) **non-iodized salt**
2 cups (500 ml) **soy sauce**
1 cup (250 ml) **water**
½ tsp (2 ml) **onion powder**
½ tsp (2 ml) **garlic powder**
½ tsp (2 ml) **pepper**
½ tsp (2 ml) **Tabasco sauce**
1 cup (250 ml) dry white **wine**

Method:
In a glass, stainless steel or food-grade plastic, combine all ingredients in a large container. Brine salmon, or any fish for smoking, 8 or more hours in refrigerator. Rinse, pat dry and smoke 12 hours or less, with the larger chunks on bottom.

Vittorio's Salmon Brine

Contributed by Jeanette Cazzola, Sidney, B.C., Canada

Ingredients:
- 3 cups (750 ml) **water**
- 1 cup (250 ml) dry white **wine**
- 1 cup (250 ml) **soy sauce**
- Dash **Tabasco sauce**
- ½ cup (125 ml) **salt**
- ½ cup (125 ml) **white sugar**
- ½ cup (125 ml) **brown sugar**
- ½ tsp (2 ml) **garlic powder**
- ½ tsp (2 ml) **onion powder**

Method:

In a glass, stainless steel or food-grade plastic, combine all ingredients. Marinate salmon, or any fish for smoking, overnight in the refrigerator. Drain, rinse and pat dry. Smoke 4 hours using 4 trays of chips, changing chips each hour.

Fred's Brine for Smoking Salmon

Ingredients:
- ½ cup (125 ml) coarse **salt**
- ½ cup (125 ml) **brown sugar**
- ¼ cup (60 ml) **molasses**
- 4 cups (1 l) **water**
- **Brown sugar** for rub

Method:

In a glass, stainless steel or food-grade plastic, combine first 4 ingredients. Soak fish in brine for five hours in the refrigerator. Wash fish in fresh water and pat dry. Leave out in air to dry one hour. Rub with brown sugar before smoking.

Clams

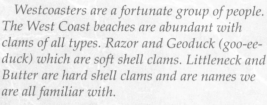

Westcoasters are a fortunate group of people. The West Coast beaches are abundant with clams of all types. Razor and Geoduck (goo-ee-duck) which are soft shell clams. Littleneck and Butter are hard shell clams and are names we are all familiar with.

Razor clams are cleaned as soon as possible after digging. To remove the meat from the shell, run a knife blade along the inner side of shell to cut the muscles holding the shells together. Clean clams by cutting off the black tip of the neck. Insert scissors into the neck and cut clam lengthwise from the tip of the neck to the base of the foot. Remove the gills and digestive tract (the dark parts of the clam) and discard. Cut the digger foot so it will lie flat, pick out the small intestine that runs through the foot and rinse free of any sand. The Razor clam may also be steamed open as in Little Neck clams below.

The Geoduck, a very large clam, is generally used as steaks or ground up for fritters and chowders. Thoroughly wash the clam. Remove meat from shell as for Razor clams above. Remove the neck (siphon) from the body of the clam. Although all of the Geoduck can be eaten, the neck is the choice part and generally the only part eaten. Quickly blanch the neck in boiling water. Remove the skin from the neck and rinse in cold water. The meat may now be either cut into slices for steaks or ground for cakes, fritters or chowder. Steaks should be quickly fried in butter. Do not overcook the steaks as it toughens the meat.

Littleneck clams are best steamed. Prepare the clams by scrubbing under cold running water to remove sand. Place the washed clams in a bucket of clean water to which ½ cup (125 ml) of salt has been added. Let them stand for a few hours; they clean themselves of any internal sand. If you are cooking your freshly dug clams on the beach, put them in a bucket of fresh sea water and let them stand for about 20 minutes. They will clean themselves in this way. To steam the Littlenecks place them in a steamer or a large kettle with about an inch (2.5 cm) of water in the bottom. Cover tightly and steam for about 5 minutes for small clams and up to 10 minutes for larger ones or until shells are partially open. Serve clams on the half-shell along with the strained liquor and melted butter or use the meat in your favorite recipe. When cooking, in the shell, discard any clams that do not open!

Clam Griddle Cakes with Cran-Applesauce

Ingredients:
- 2 cans (5 oz / 142 g) **clams**, minced and undrained
- 1 ½ cups (375 ml) **clam liquor** and / or **milk**
- 1 ½ cups (375 ml) **flour**
- 1 cup (250 ml) yellow **corn meal**
- 5 tsp (25 ml) **baking powder**
- **Salt** to taste
- 2 **eggs**, beaten
- ⅓ cup (80 ml) **oil**
- **Butter** OR **margarine**
- **Cran-Applesauce** (recipe follows)

Method:
Drain clams and measure clam liquor, adding enough milk to make 1 ½ cups (375 ml). In another bowl, sift together flour, corn meal, baking powder and salt. In a separate bowl, mix together beaten eggs, oil and minced clams. Add flour mixture to clam liquor alternating with the egg mixture. Stir just until blended. Drop ¼ cup (60 ml) - ½ cup (125 ml) of batter onto a hot, well-greased griddle or fry pan. Fry 1-2 minutes per side. Serve with sauce and butter.

Cran-Applesauce

Ingredients:
- 1 can (14 oz / 398 ml) jellied **cranberry sauce**
- ½ cup (125 ml) **applesauce**
- 1 tsp (5 ml) **cinnamon** OR to taste

Method:
In a medium size bowl, blend all ingredients thoroughly. Chill.

21

Scalloped Clams

Ingredients:
- 2 cups (500 ml) **cracker crumbs**, crushed
- ½ tsp (2 ml) **salt**
- ½ cup (125 ml) **butter** OR **margarine**
- 1 pt (500 ml) fresh **clams**, chopped, drained, reserve liquor
- ¼ tsp (1 ml) **Worcestershire sauce**
- 1 cup (250 ml) **clam liquor**, extended with **milk** if needed
- Dash **pepper**

Method:

Coat a casserole dish with non-stick cooking spray. Combine cracker crumbs, salt and butter. Spread ⅓ of cracker mixture on the bottom of the casserole dish. Spread half of the clams on top of the crackers; repeat layers reserving about ¼ cup (60 ml) crumbs. Mix Worcestershire sauce with clam liquor/milk and pour over layers. Sprinkle with remaining crumbs. Bake in a 350°F (180°C) oven for 30 minutes and browned on top. Serves 6.

Clam Hors d'oeuvres

Ingredients:
- 1 can cream of celery **soup**
- ¼ cup (60 ml) **clam nectar**
- ½ pt. (250 ml) fresh **clams**, chopped
- ¼ cup (60 ml) dry **bread crumbs**, finely crushed
- **Salt** and **pepper** to taste
- 1 ½ tsp (7 ml) **Parmesan cheese**
- 1 ½ tsp (7 ml) **parsley**
- ½ tsp (2 ml) **paprika**
- Collect shells that are 2 inches (5 cm) across and scrub clean.

Method:

In a medium-size bowl, mix together soup, nectar, clams, crumbs, salt and pepper. Spoon mixture into clam shells. Place shells on cookie sheet over a bed of rock salt about ½" (1 cm) deep or crumble some tin foil and place around shells to keep from moving around. Sprinkle with the Parmesan cheese, parsley and paprika. Bake in a 325°F (160°C) oven for 20 minutes or until bubbly and golden brown. Makes 2 dozen hors d'oeuvres.

Roasted Clams

Ingredients:
   6 lbs (3 kg) **clams**
   Butter, melted

Method:
   Scrub clam shells well. Place shells with the deep side of the shell down in order to hold the juices, on a cookie sheet. To keep shells from moving around, crumble up tin foil and place around shells. Roast in a 450°F (230°C) oven until shells open, approximately 4-8 minutes depending on the thickness of the shell. (Caution, shells are very hot!). Serve the clams, in the shell, with melted butter for dipping. Discard any clam shells that did not open.

Super Clam Canapés

Ingredients:
   1 can (7 oz / 199 ml) minced **clams**, drained
   1 pkg (3 oz / 85 g) **cream cheese** with chives, softened
   ½ tsp (2 ml) **salt** or to taste
   1 Tbsp (15 ml) **lemon juice**
   3 drops **Tabasco sauce**
   1 **egg white**, stiffly beaten
   Crackers OR **toast**
   Paprika

Method:
   Combine clams, cream cheese and seasonings. Fold in beaten egg white. Spread resulting mixture onto crackers or toast and sprinkle with paprika. Broil 3 inches (7.5 cm) from heat source for 2-3 minutes or until golden brown. Makes 36 canapés.

Cod

The codfish are probably the most economically important fish in the world. They are found in both the Atlantic and Pacific oceans. We, on the West Coast, are more familiar with the Pacific Cod. The cod should be gutted and chilled quickly for the best flavor. To buy fresh cod fillets, they should be sweet smelling and snowy white flesh. Make sure there are no brown spots or dryness showing signs of aging.

How to tell when your fish is cooked? Follow recipe directions and just before the allotted time, check your fish by poking with a fork in the thickest part. Perfectly cooked fish is almost opaque and flakes easily when tested with a fork. It should also be very moist looking. Two exceptions of this rule are tuna and salmon, if your fish is very fresh, both can be served rare in the centre.

Try cod deep-fried for fish and chips with malt vinegar for a traditional dinner. Cod steaks are delicious grilled. Remove the small bones from fillets before cooking. And for a wonderful soup stock cook the heads and bones, see soup stock recipe on page 150.

Dad's Fresh Fish Burgers

Contributed by Gordon Hood, Ashcroft, B.C., Canada

Ingredients:

2 cups (500 ml) **water**
1 lb (454 g) fresh **cod**, cut
   into small pieces
1 **egg**, beaten
½ cup (125 ml) **bread**
   crumbs, dried, crushed
½ tsp (2 ml) dried **dill**
   weed
½ tsp (2 ml) **lemon rind**,
   grated
¼ cup (60 ml) fresh
   parsley, chopped fine
1 ½ tsp (7 ml) dry **mustard**
1 Tbsp (15 ml) **Seafood**
   sauce
Salt and **pepper** to taste
Oil for frying
Buns

Method:

In medium size saucepan, bring water to boil. Add fish, cover and simmer turning once, until fish flakes when tested with a fork, approximately 5 minutes. Drain and cool fish. In a large bowl, mash fish and combine with beaten egg, add remainder of ingredients (other than oil and buns) mixing well. Divide into 4 patties, approximately ½ inch (1 cm) thick. Heat oil over medium high heat in large heavy fry pan, cook patties, turning once, until golden and firm, about 10 minutes. Serve with Tartar Sauce, see recipe on page 12.

Salted Codfish Cakes

Ingredients:

1 lb (454 g) **salt cod**, cut into serving-size pieces

6 medium **potatoes**, peeled

3 green **onions**, sliced

3 Tbsp (45 ml) **parsley**, finely chopped

¼ cup (60 ml) fresh **cilantro**, chopped (optional)

1 Tbsp (15 ml) **butter**

Pinch **pepper**

Pinch **nutmeg**

Milk (optional)

Butter for frying (optional)

Corn flakes, crushed (optional)

Method:

To reduce saltiness and freshen salt cod, place in large, deep glass bowl, cover fish with cold water and with plastic wrap. Let soak overnight in refrigerator. Drain, rinse well when ready to use. (If still too salty, continue changing water and soak for another 3-4 hours.) Place fish in saucepan and add enough water to cover. Simmer until fish flakes when fork-tested, about 10 minutes. Drain and let cool before removing bones. Flake fish. Cook potatoes until tender. Mash potatoes and combine with flaked fish, onion, parsley, cilantro, butter, pepper and nutmeg. Shape resulting mixture into cakes. Beat in a small amount of milk, if necessary, to make handling easier. Fish cakes may be cooked the traditional way by frying in butter over medium heat, about 2-3 minutes per side, until crisp and golden brown. Or, fish cakes may also be coated with corn flakes, placed in greased muffin pans and baked in 350°F (180°C) oven for 20 minutes. Serves 6.

Kamaboko Fish Patties

Ingredients:

1 ½ cups (375 ml) fresh
  cod OR **salmon**
½ tsp (2 ml) **baking soda**
3 tsp (15 ml) **sugar**
½ tsp (2 ml) **Accent**
  (optional)
1 **egg**, lightly beaten
1 tsp (5 ml) **Mirin**
  (Japanese sweet white
  Saki)
2 tsp (10 ml) **sesame seeds**,
  roasted
½ cup (125 ml) or more
  carrots, minced
2 green **onions**, chopped
  fine
2 Tbsp (30 ml) **corn starch**
1 tsp (5 ml) **rye** OR **sherry**
¼ cup (60 ml) (scant)
  canned **evaporated milk**
2 tsp (10 ml) **salt** or to taste

Method:

Fish should be kept in refrigerator and be at least 1 day old. If necessary, fillet fish and remove skin. Cut into narrow strips and whirl in blender until very smooth. In a medium-size bowl knead together fish and baking soda. Add sugar, Accent, egg, and Mirin. Knead until well blended. Add sesame seeds, carrots and onions. Knead well again. Add corn starch, rye or sherry, and milk. Knead until smooth. Add salt and knead until slightly firm. Shape into patties and deep fry in 350°F (180°C) oil until patties puff up and are golden brown. They will settle when cooled. For those watching their fat intake, these patties may be steamed. To test for doneness, insert a toothpick in center, patties are cooked when it comes out clean.

A new study suggests you may improve your eyesight by eating more fish!

27

Favorite Cod on Greens

Ingredients:
- ¼ cup (60 ml) **parsley**, chopped
- 1 tsp (5 ml) **garlic**, minced
- ½ tsp (2 ml) **orange peel**, grated
- ½ tsp (2 ml) ground black **pepper**
- ¼ tsp (1 ml) **salt**
- 1 Tbsp (15 ml) extra-virgin **olive oil**
- 1 lb (454 g) **cod** fillet, cut into quarters
- ½ cup (125 ml) dry **bread crumbs**, crushed fine
- **Lemon** OR **orange** slices

Method:
In a bowl combine parsley, garlic, orange peel, pepper, salt, and oil. Dip cod in this mixture and pat on bread crumbs. Place cod in lightly oiled 13 inch x 9 inch (34 cm x 22 cm) baking dish and place in a 400°F (200°C) oven for 10-12 minutes or until opaque throughout and fish flakes when fork-tested. Lay cod on a bed of greens (recipe following) on a warm serving platter and garnish with lemon and/or orange slices.

Greens

Ingredients:
- 2 slices **bacon**, reserve drippings
- 1 tsp (5 ml) **garlic**, minced
- Pinch ground red **pepper**
- 2 lbs (1 kg) **spinach** OR other favorite **greens**, washed

Method:
Cook bacon until crisp, drain on paper towel. Reserve 1 Tbsp (15 ml) drippings. Crumble bacon and return to pan with garlic and red pepper; cook for 15 seconds. Increase heat and add spinach or other greens to pan and cook quickly until just beginning to wilt.

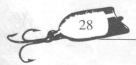

Cod Provençal

Ingredients:
- 1 large **onion**, chopped, about 1 cup (250 ml)
- 1 **clove garlic**, minced
- 1 cup (250 ml) **mushrooms**, sliced (optional)
- 3 Tbsp (45 ml) vegetable **oil**
- 2 large ripe **tomatoes**, chopped
- 1 tsp (5 ml) **salt** or to taste
- 1 tsp (5 ml) leaf **thyme**, crumbled
- ¼ tsp (1 ml) **pepper**
- 1 lb (454 g) **cod** fillets, fresh or frozen

Method:
In a large heavy fry pan, sauté onion, garlic and mushrooms in vegetable oil until tender. Add tomatoes and cook 2 minutes. Add salt, thyme and pepper. Place fresh or frozen cod fillets into sauce, spooning part of the sauce over the fillets. Cover and simmer for 15 minutes or until fish just begins to flake when fork-tested. Place cooked fillets on warm serving platter spooning any remaining sauce over fish. If you like, surround fish with small boiled red potatoes and garnish with cucumber slices and parsley.

Italian Baked Cod

Ingredients:
- 1 ½ lbs (750 g) **cod** fillet
- 1 can (14 oz/398 ml) Italian-style stewed **tomatoes**, undrained
- 1 Tbsp (15 ml) **capers**, drained and/OR 12-16 pitted black **olives** OR pimento-stuffed green **olives**
- 1-2 Tbsp (15-30 ml) **Parmesan cheese**, grated

Method:
Preheat oven to 375°F (190°C). Rinse fish, pat dry. Place fillets in greased baking dish, tucking thin tail ends under so fillets are even thickness. Pour tomatoes over fish. Sprinkle with capers and/or olives. Sprinkle Parmesan cheese over all. Bake fish uncovered until opaque in center and flakes easily, about 20-25 minutes for fillets about 1 inch (2.5 cm) thick. Serve with rice Serves 4.

Cod Roll-Ups

Ingredients:
  1 lb (454 g) **cod** fillets
  Tartar Sauce
  Cheese slices
  1 can (8 oz / 227 ml) **tomato sauce**
  ½ can (4 oz / 114 ml) **water**
  1 tsp (5 ml) **curry powder** (optional)
  Bread crumbs, dry, crushed fine
  Butter

Method:
  Slice fillets to about ¼ inch (.5 cm) thick. Spread with Tartar sauce and place a cheese slice onto the fillet. Roll up and secure with a wooden toothpick. Place rolled fillets into a greased baking dish, seam side down. Combine tomato sauce, water and curry powder and pour over fillets. Sprinkle with bread crumbs and dot each roll with butter. Bake in a 375°F (190°C) oven for 20-30 minutes or until fish flakes when fork-tested.

Cod Au Gratin

Ingredients:
  4 Tbsp (60 ml) **butter** OR **margarine**
  2 Tbsp (30 ml) **flour**
  2 cups (500 ml) **milk**
  Salt and **pepper** to taste
  2 ½ cups (625 ml) **cod**, cooked, flaked, cooled
  1 cup (250 ml) **cheese**, grated

Method:
  Melt butter in heavy fry pan over medium heat. Blend in flour. Cook 3 minutes until flour is absorbed, stirring occasionally. Slowly add milk, stirring constantly to prevent lumps, until mixture boils and thickens. Season with salt and pepper. In lightly greased 9" (23 cm) baking dish add a layer of fish, alternating layers with sauce. Sprinkle top with shredded cheese. Bake in a 350°F (175°C) oven for 15 minutes or until cheese is browned.

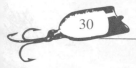

Sweet and Sour Cod Fillets

Contributed by Karin Hardy, Prince George, B.C., Canada

Ingredients:

- ½ cup (125 ml) **water**
- ¼ cup (60 ml) cider **vinegar**
- 1 tsp (5 ml) **corn starch**
- 2 Tbsp (30 ml) **honey**
- ¼ tsp (1 ml) fresh **ginger**, peeled and grated
- 2 **cloves garlic**
- 2 Tbsp (30 ml) **tomato paste**
- 1 Tbsp (15 ml) **lemon juice** (optional)
- 1 ½ lbs (750 g) **cod** fillets
- 2 **scallions**, thinly sliced lengthwise OR
  2 Tbsp (30 ml) **chives**, chopped (garnish)

Method:

Place the water, vinegar and corn starch in a small saucepan and stir until the corn starch is dissolved. Over low heat add the honey and ginger. Put the garlic through a garlic press into the pan. Stir in the tomato paste. Bring to a boil, reduce heat, and simmer for 10 minutes, stirring occasionally. Remove from heat and set aside keeping warm until ready to use.

Meanwhile, as the sauce simmers, place ½ inch (1 cm) of water in a large skillet. Put in lemon juice, if desired. Bring to a boil. Reduce heat to a slow simmer and gently add the cod. Cover and poach the fish for 8-10 minutes or until opaque throughout and fish flakes easily when fork tested. Remove fish and place on a warm serving platter. Spoon the sweet and sour sauce on top of the fish. Garnish with scallions, if desired.

Cod with Herb Tomato Sauce

Ingredients:

1 Tbsp (15 ml) **olive oil**
¼ cup (60 ml) **onion**, finely chopped
1 tsp (5 ml) **garlic**, minced
1 can (14 oz/398 ml) **tomatoes**
Salt to taste
⅛ tsp (.5 ml) **thyme**
2 Tbsp (30 ml) **parsley**, chopped
1 ½ lbs (750 g) **cod** fillets, cut into 1" (2.5 cm) pieces
3 Tbsp (45 ml) **parsley**, chopped
1 Tbsp (15 ml) extra-virgin **olive oil**
½ tsp (2 ml) **garlic**, minced
Salt and **pepper** to taste

Method:

To make tomato sauce, heat olive oil in a skillet over medium heat. Add onion and cook until transparent, about 3 minutes. Add garlic and stir for 10-15 seconds. Add tomatoes, salt and thyme. Break up tomatoes while cooking over high heat until thick. Remove from heat, stir in parsley and set aside keeping warm until ready to use.

Arrange cod in a shallow microwaveable dish. In a small bowl combine parsley, oil, garlic, salt and pepper. Spread mixture over the fish. Cover dish with wax paper and cook in microwave on HIGH 6-8 minutes or until fish flakes when fork-tested. To serve, spread sauce on a warm serving platter, arrange fish on top and sprinkle with more chopped parsley for garnish if desired. Serves 4.

SEAFOOD

Traditional Fish & Chips 33

Cod with Herb
Tomato Sauce 32

Favorite Cod
on Greens 28

Cod Roll-Ups 30

Cod Provencal 29

Traditional Fish & Chips

Ingredients:
  2 lbs (1 kg) fresh or frozen
    cod OR **halibut**, cut into
    serving size pieces
  Oil for deep frying
  Lemon juice
  1 cup (250 ml) sifted all-
    purpose **flour**
  1 tsp (5 ml) **salt**
  3 tsp (15 ml) **paprika**
  1 cup (250 ml) **beer**
  Flour

Method:
  If using frozen fish, thaw
until easily separated. Rinse
fish under cold running water
and pat dry. Fill a deep-fat fryer
or deep heavy saucepan ⅓ full
with oil. Heat to 375°F (190°C).
Sprinkle fish lightly with lemon
juice. In a medium-size mixing
bowl combine the flour, salt
and paprika, gradually add the
beer, beating until batter is well
blended and smooth. Put a little
flour into a flat dish and coat
fish evenly on both sides. Coat
fish with batter, let excess batter
drip off and gently drop into
hot oil. Fry until batter is a deep
golden brown, about 5-7
minutes. Fish should be moist,
opaque and flake easily when
fork-tested. For a traditional
dinner serve with chips (french
fries) and malt vinegar. Serves
4-6.

"Studies show that eating seafood twice a week can help keep your well-being at its peak."

Rocky Point Creamy Pureed Cod

Ingredients:
1 qt (1 l) **milk**
1 small **onion**, minced
4 Tbsp (60 ml) **butter**
4 Tbsp (60 ml) **flour**
2 tsp (10 ml) **salt**
⅛ tsp (.5 ml) **pepper**
2 cups (500 ml) **cod**, cooked
Parsley OR **paprika**

Method:
In a small pot, scald the milk and onion. In a heavy fry pan over medium heat, melt butter, blend in the flour, salt and pepper, cook 2-3 minutes until flour absorbed. Slowly add scalded milk, stirring constantly to prevent lumps, until mixture boils and thickens. Put fish through a sieve and add to sauce. Garnish with chopped parsley or paprika. Serve over noodles. Serves 6.

Chinese Braised Cod

Contributed by Mae Hood, Parksville, B.C., Canada

Ingredients:
1-1 ½ lbs (454-750 g) **cod***
½ tsp (2 ml) **salt**
⅛ tsp (.5 ml) **pepper**
2 tsp (10 ml) **oil**
½ cup (125 ml) **mushrooms**, sliced
2 green **onions**, sliced
4 water **chestnuts**
½ tsp (2 ml) fresh **ginger**, peeled and diced
1 **clove garlic**, crushed
¾ cup (175 ml) fish OR chicken **stock**
1 Tbsp (15 ml) **soy sauce**
2 tsp (10 ml) **lemon juice**

Method:
Sprinkle fish with salt and pepper. Heat oil in a hot skillet and sear fish until golden brown on both sides. Add remaining ingredients to skillet, stir. Cover and simmer 15-20 minutes or until fish flakes when fork-tested. Turn fish over during cooking. Serve with sauce over fish. Serves 2.
*Can be used with any firm white fish.

Crab

Crab! Just the name brings visions of mouth-watering eating around a beach fire, gourmet dinners aboard a yacht or just plain good eating at home. Crab! The Northwest is famous for its large succulent crab.

As an alternative to catching your own crab, you can buy live whole or cooked crab, cooked legs, canned crab, flaked meat which is light and dark meat from the claws and the body, and lumpmeat which is cooked white pieces from the body of the crab. If you decide to buy whole cooked crabs, look for ones that have bright red shells. Or, if you want live crabs, pick out ones that are active. The recipes in this book bring out the naturally sweet flavor of the tender meat.

How to Cook Crab

1. Place the live crab in enough salted boiling water (¼ cup/60 ml) salt per 1 gallon (4 l) to cover it. You may want to kill the crab first by striking through the backside of the live crab with a small hatchet (don't cut through the upper shell). Break out the body sections and clean. Immerse immediately in boiling water.

2. Cook the crabs at a rolling boil for approximately 5-8 minutes per pound e.g., 12 minutes for a 1 ½ lb (750 g) crab. Crabs will turn a bright pinkish-orange color when cooked.

3. Or, if you want to just cook one crab, cook in boiling, salted water for about 5 minutes. Crabs will turn a bright pinkish-orange color when cooked.

4. Immediately plunge the cooked crab into cold water, until the shell is cool, in order to stop the cooking process. To over-cook the crabs results in a tougher meat.

How to Clean Crab

1. Remove the back shell. Hold the base of the crab with one hand and its back shell with the other, thumbs at the center back. Lift off the shell.

2. Remove and discard the viscera (the semi-liquid material in the body cavity) and the feathery gills.

3. Rinse the crab thoroughly under cool, running water to wash away all loose material.

4. Grasp the crab in both hands and break it in half. Separate the legs from each other, leaving a portion of the body connected to each for easy handling.

5. Crack the shell of each leg with a small meat mallet or nut cracker, or use kitchen shears to cut through the shell. Break back the shell to expose the meat. Remove the meat using the tip of a leg or small pick or fork.

6. To remove meat from claws, break each from leg joint and crack. Break off small pincer by pulling it back and out. Use this 'pick' to remove meat from shell.

Crab Casserole

Ingredients:
- 3 cups (750 ml) **zucchini**, sliced
- 1 **onion**, sliced
- 1 **clove garlic**
- ¼ tsp (1 ml) **basil**
- ¼ tsp (1 ml) **pepper**
- **Paprika** to taste (optional)
- 2 Tbsp (30 ml) **butter**
- 1 can (8 oz / 225 g) **crab meat**
- 1 can cream of mushroom **soup**
- 3 cups (750 ml) cooked **rice**
- ½ lb (225 g) Cheddar **cheese**, grated
- ½ cup (125 ml) **Parmesan cheese**

Method:
In a fry pay, sauté zucchini, onion, garlic and seasonings in butter until soft and translucent. Remove garlic clove. Add crab, soup, rice and cheddar cheese, stir until blended. Pour into a buttered casserole and sprinkle Parmesan cheese over the top. Sprinkle paprika over cheese. Cover and bake in a 350°F (180°C) oven for 20 minutes. Remove cover and bake 5 minutes more or until golden brown.

Deviled Crab

Contributed by Hazel Campbell, Abbotsford, B.C., Canada

Ingredients:
- 3 fresh **crabs**
- 1 cup (250 ml) dry **bread crumbs**, crushed fine
- 2 **eggs**, beaten
- 1 cup (250 ml) canned **milk**
- ½ tsp (2 ml) **Tabasco sauce**
- Poultry **seasoning** to taste
- Few flakes dried **onion**

Method:
Remove meat from crab, discard cartilage, add to the rest of the ingredients. Mix, place in greased casserole dish. Bake about 30-45 minutes at 350°F (180°C) or until knife comes out clean from center. Can also be baked on clean scrubbed shells surrounded by crumbled tin foil. Shorten baking time to 15-20 minutes or until toothpick comes out clean from center.

37

Oriental Crab Cakes

Ingredients:
 4 **eggs**
 ½ tsp (2 ml) **salt**
 ¼ tsp (1 ml) ground **ginger**
 1 cup (250 ml) cooked
   crab*
 2 green **onions**, finely
   chopped
 1 stalk **celery**, thinly sliced
 2 cups (500 ml) canned or
   fresh bean **sprouts**
 1-2 Tbsp (15-30 ml) **butter**
   OR vegetable **oil**
 *You can substitute
   cooked **shrimp** OR other
   seafood for the **crab**.

Method:
 In a medium-size bowl, beat
together eggs, salt and ginger.
Stir in crab, onion, celery and
bean sprouts until well
blended. In a 9 inch (23 cm)
non-stick skillet heat 1 Tbsp
(15 ml) of the butter or oil. Place
¼ cup (60 ml) of mixture into
hot oil and flatten with a
spatula to form patties about
½ inch (1.5 cm) thick. Cook for
2-3 minutes on each side or
until golden brown. Keep
patties warm until all are
cooked. Serve with Lemon
Sauce on page 11.

Crab Alfredo

Ingredients:
 1 pkg noodles, **fettuccine**
 ½ cup (125 ml) **cream cheese**
 ½ cup (125 ml) **butter**
 ⅔ cup (150 ml) **Parmesan**
   cheese, grated
 1 cup (250 ml) **milk**
 ½ tsp (2 ml) **garlic powder**
 ¼ cup (60 ml) **mushrooms**,
   sliced
 2 Tbsp (30 ml) green **onions**,
   sliced
 ¾ cup (175 ml) cooked **crab**

Method:
 Cook pasta according to
package directions.
Meanwhile, in a saucepan
over low heat, mix together
cream cheese, butter and
Parmesan cheese. Slowly stir
in milk until smooth. Season
with garlic powder. In a small
fry pan, sauté mushrooms
and green onions, add to
sauce. Just before serving,
add crab, heat through. Serve
sauce over cooked noodles.

Crab Quesadillas with Salsa

Ingredients:
- ½ lb (225 g) **crab meat**, fresh-cooked or canned
- 2 green **onions**, chopped
- 4 oz (115 g) Jack **cheese** OR Cheddar **cheese**, grated
- 6 **flour tortillas**
- ½ cup (125 ml) red OR green **salsa**

Method:
Preheat oven to 400°F (200°C). In a medium-size bowl mix crab, onions, and cheese together. Lay tortilla flat and spoon equal amounts of crab mixture on each. Spread to within ½ inch (1 cm) of the edge on one half of tortilla. Fold tortilla in half enclosing filling. Lay on a baking sheet and bake until cheese melts, about 5 minutes. Cut tortillas into wedges, spoon salsa over top.

Individual Crab Casseroles

Ingredients:
- 2 lbs (1 kg) **crab**, cooked OR 6 cans (6 ½ oz / 175 ml ea)
- 1 cup (250 ml) **sour cream**
- ⅓ cup (80 ml) **Parmesan cheese**, grated
- 1 Tbsp (15 ml) **lemon juice**
- 1 Tbsp (15 ml) **onion**, grated
- ½ tsp (2 ml) **salt**
- Dash **Tabasco**
- 1 Tbsp (15 ml) melted **bacon** fat or any **oil**
- ¾ cup (175 ml) soft **bread**, cubed
- **Paprika**

Method:
Place crab in a bowl. In a separate bowl, combine and thoroughly mix next 6 ingredients. Pour sauce over crab, mix lightly. Place crab mixture in 6 well-greased shells (if using shells, rumple tin foil up and place around shells on a cookie sheet to keep them upright) or custard cups. Pour melted fat over bread cubes, mix until coated. Spread over crab mixture and sprinkle with Paprika. Bake in a 350°F (180°C) oven for 15-20 minutes until lightly browned. Serves 6.

39

Open-Face Broiled Crab Sandwiches

Ingredients:
- 4 English **muffins**
- 1 can (6 oz/170 g) **crab**, drained and flaked
- ½ cup (125 ml) **sour cream**
- ½ cup (125 ml) **mayonnaise**
- 2 Tbsp (30 ml) green **onion**, chopped

Method:

Slice muffins in half and broil cut sides only. Spread crabmeat over each half. Combine sour cream, mayonnaise and green onion. Cover crab with this mixture. Broil 3 inches (7.5 cm) from heat source until golden brown. Serve hot with a garden salad. Serves 4.

Crab and Bacon Fingers

Ingredients:
- 1 **egg**
- ¼ cup (60 ml) **tomato juice**
- 1 can (7 ½ oz/213 g) OR 1 cup (250 ml) cooked **crab meat**, drained and flaked
- ½ cup (125 ml) dry **bread crumbs**, finely crushed
- 1 Tbsp (15 ml) **parsley**, chopped
- 1 Tbsp (15 ml) **lemon juice**
- ¼ tsp (1 ml) **Worcestershire sauce**
- Dash **pepper**
- 9 slices **bacon**

Method:

In a small bowl beat egg, add tomato juice and mix well. Add crab, crumbs, parsley, lemon juice, Worcestershire sauce, and pepper and mix thoroughly. Pat or roll equal portions of mixture into 18 fingers about 2 inches (5 cm) long. Cut bacon in half, wrap around each finger and fasten with a wooden toothpick. Place on a broiling pan, pick side down. Broil about 5 inches (12.5 cm) from heat source about 10 minutes or until bacon is cooked. Turn often so fingers brown evenly. Makes 18 fingers.

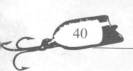

Crab on Garlic Toast

Ingredients:
- 2 Tbsp (30 ml) **butter**
- 1 medium-size **onion**, finely minced
- ½ cup (125 ml) **milk**
- 1 cup (250 ml) cooked **rice**
- 1 cup (250 ml) canned OR cooked, flaked **crab meat**
- 2 fresh **tomatoes**, skinned and quartered
- ⅓ cup (80 ml) **butter**
- ½ **clove garlic**
- 12 slices **bread**
- **Paprika**

Method:
Melt butter in a skillet and slowly brown onion. Add milk, rice and crab; heat together gently. Add tomatoes and cook just until they are heated through. In a small saucepan melt butter with the garlic clove. When hot, remove garlic, brush bread with seasoned butter. Toast. Sprinkle with paprika. Cut into halves or quarters. Spoon crab mixture over toast and serve hot.

Cocktail Seafood Salad

Ingredients:
- 2 ripe **avocados**
- 2 Tbsp (30 ml) **lemon juice**
- ½ tsp (2 ml) seasoned **salt**
- ¼ tsp (1 ml) lemon **pepper**
- 2 stalks **celery**, chopped
- 2 green **onions** with tops, sliced
- 1 Tbsp (15 ml) **parsley**, chopped
- 5 oz (142 ml) water **chestnuts**, chopped
- 1 can (6 oz / 170 g) **crab** OR **shrimp**
- Cocktail or chili **sauce**
- **Cashews**

Method:
Cut avocado lengthwise, remove pit. Scoop out avocado with a melon baller or a 1 tsp (5 ml) measuring spoon to make balls. Toss balls in lemon juice. To avocado balls mix in seasoned salt, lemon pepper, celery, onions, parsley and water chestnuts. Place mixture in individual shells or on a serving plate, add seafood. Top with sauce, sprinkle with cashews.

41

Microwaved Crab Fettuccine

Ingredients:
- 1 Tbsp (15 ml) **olive oil**
- 1 lb (454 g) dry **spinach** OR tomato **fettuccine**
- 2 Tbsp (30 ml) **butter** OR **margarine**
- 4 **mushrooms**, chopped
- 1 **clove garlic**, minced
- 8 oz (225 g) fresh cooked lumped **crabmeat** OR canned and drained
- 1 cup (250 ml) **whipping cream**
- ¼ tsp (1 ml) **salt**
- ¼ tsp (1 ml) white **pepper**
- ¼ tsp (1 ml) powdered **saffron**
- ⅔ cup (150 ml) **Parmesan cheese**, grated and divided
- 2 tsp (10 ml) fresh **dill**, finely chopped OR ⅔ tsp (3 ml) dried **dill weed**

Method:

Bring a large pot of water to boil. Add oil and the dry pasta; cook to al denté stage (firm to the bite); drain well. In a medium-size, microwave safe bowl, heat butter on HIGH for 45 seconds; add mushrooms and garlic; stir. Continue cooking on HIGH for 2 more minutes stirring once. Add crabmeat, cover bowl loosely with waxed paper and cook on HIGH 2-3 minutes until hot. Mix the cream into the crab mixture and heat on MEDIUM power for 2-3 minutes, until cream begins to bubble. Whisk in seasonings. Combine sauce with pasta, tossing to mix. Add ½ cup (125 ml) of the Parmesan cheese tossing to mix well. Serve on a large warmed platter. Sprinkle with remaining cheese and dill. Serves 4.

Halibut

Halibut can grow to be very large—8 feet long and up to 495 pounds! When fishermen catch one of these monsters they know they have a fish on their line. Halibut has a mild-flavored, tender-firm flesh and is available in steaks or fillets. They are delicious baked, broiled, deep-fried, butter-sautéed or poached.

To buy: Make sure the halibut is sweet smelling with pure white flesh and no signs of drying or browning.

How to tell when your fish is cooked? Follow recipe directions and just before the allotted time, check your fish by poking with a fork in the thickest part. Perfectly cooked fish is almost opaque and flakes easily when tested with a fork. It should also be very moist looking. Two exceptions of this rule are tuna and salmon, if your fish is very fresh, both can be served rare in the center.

Tangy Halibut Steaks

Contributed by Alberta Geertsma, Abbotsford, B.C., Canada

Ingredients:
2 lbs (1 kg) **halibut** steaks,
　1 inch (2.5 cm) thick
1 cup (250 ml) Italian-style
　salad dressing
1 Tbsp (15 ml) **lemon juice**
1 tsp (5 ml) **salt**
⅛ tsp (.5 ml) **pepper**
Paprika

Method:
　Cut steaks into serving size portions. Place in a single layer in a shallow dish. Combine other ingredients, except paprika. Mix well and pour over the fish. Let stand for 15 minutes, turn over and let stand another 15 minutes. Remove steaks from dish. Reserve sauce for basting. Place steaks on oiled pan, sprinkle with paprika and bake at 350°F (180°C). Bake for 8-10 minutes first side, turn, baste with marinade and bake an additional 6-8 minutes. Fish is ready when it is nicely browned, opaque and flakes when fork-tested. Place on warm serving platter and sprinkle with paprika again. Serve with Cucumber Sauce, see recipe on page 47.

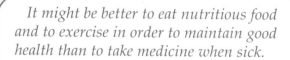

It might be better to eat nutritious food and to exercise in order to maintain good health than to take medicine when sick.

Swartz Bay Broiled Halibut Steaks

Ingredients:
4 (4-6 oz 115-170 g ea)
  halibut steaks
2 Tbsp (30 ml) melted
  butter OR **olive oil**
2 Tbsp (30 ml) **lemon juice**
Fresh **dill** OR **parsley**
  sprigs
Lemon wedges

Method:
Lightly grease a broiler pan. Place steaks on pan and brush with melted butter or oil. Drizzle with lemon juice. Broil steaks 4-6 inch (10-15 cm) from the heat source, for 6 minutes on first side, turn, baste with marinade and broil for about another 6 minutes or until the fish flakes when fork-tested, is opaque and nicely browned. Place steaks on warmed serving platter. Garnish with dill or parsley and lemon wedges. Serves 4.

Halibut Neptune

Contributed by LeAnne Bowden, Ladysmith, B.C., Canada

Ingredients:
4 oz (115 g) **cream cheese**,
  softened
2 tsp (10 ml) **lemon juice**
¼-½ tsp (1-2 ml) **salt**
⅛ tsp (.5 ml) **pepper**
½ tsp (2 ml) **parsley** and/or
  your own combo of herbs
¼ cup (60 ml) **shrimp** and/
  or **crab**, cooked
2 **halibut** fillets
  (7 oz/200g ea)

Method:
In a small bowl, mix cheese, lemon juice, salt, pepper, parsley and until well blended. Add shrimp and crab, gently stir. Place halibut in shallow baking dish. Spread cream cheese mixture over halibut. Bake in 350°F (180°C) oven until halibut flakes when fork-tested, approximately 12-15 minutes.

Halibut Sauté

Ingredients:

3 Tbsp (45 ml) teriyaki **sauce**

3 Tbsp (45 ml) **water**

2 tsp (10 ml) **corn starch**

½ fresh **lemon**, juiced and rind, grated

1 tsp (5 ml) fresh **ginger**, peeled and grated

1 **clove garlic**, minced

1 lb (454 g) **halibut** fillet

3 Tbsp (45 ml) **oil**, divided

1 cup (250 ml) **carrots**, sliced

1 cup (250 ml) green bell **pepper**, sliced

1 cup (250 ml) green **onion**, sliced

1 cup (250 ml) **broccoli** flowerets

Method:

Mix teriyaki sauce, water, corn starch, lemon juice and rind, ginger and garlic together in a small bowl. Set aside. Cut fish into 1 inch (2.5 cm) cubes and sauté in 2 Tbsp (30 ml) oil until barely cooked but lightly browned. Remove fish from skillet and set aside. In same pan or wok, with more oil if needed, sauté vegetables until tender-crisp. Add sauce. Cook and stir until sauce thickens. Return fish to vegetables and heat 1-2 minutes or until fish flakes when fork-tested. Serves 4.

Halibut with Cucumber Sauce

Ingredients:
- 3 cups (750 ml) **water**
- ½ cup (125 ml) white **wine**
- 1 **bay leaf**
- Dash **thyme**, crushed
- 1 ½ lbs (750 g) **halibut** steaks
- **Cucumber Sauce** (recipe follows)

Method:

In a medium-size saucepan, combine water, wine, bay leaf and thyme, bring to a boil and add halibut. Reduce heat; cover and simmer for 10 minutes per inch (2.5 cm) of thickness or until steaks are opaque and flake when fork-tested. Gently remove steaks from saucepan and drain well. Serve hot or chilled with Cucumber Sauce.

Cucumber Sauce

Ingredients:
- 1 cup (250 ml) **sour cream**
- ¾ cup (175 ml) **cucumber**, finely chopped
- 1 Tbsp (15 ml) **lemon juice**
- ¼ tsp (1 ml) **dill weed**
- ¼ tsp (1 ml) **sugar**
- **Salt** and **pepper**

Method:

In a small glass bowl, gently blend all ingredients. Season with salt and pepper to taste. Place in refrigerator, covered, for at least 1 hour to blend flavors.

Many shellfish such as crabs, scallops, mussels, clams and lobsters, are actually slightly lower in cholesterol than chicken.

Halibut Shish Kebab with Pesto Sauce

Ingredients:
- 2 lbs (1 kg) fresh **halibut**, cut into 1 inch (2.5 cm) cubes
- 1 red bell **pepper**, cut into 1 inch (2.5 cm) squares, then into triangles
- 1 green bell **pepper**, cut into 1 inch (2.5 cm) squares, then into triangles
- ½ lb (225 g) small **mushrooms**, remove stems
- 1 large **onion**, cut into quarters, then sliced in half
- **Pesto basting sauce** (recipe follows)

Method:
Arrange fish and vegetables on skewers. Baste with basting sauce, cover and broil 5-6 minutes on a preheated and oiled grill. Baste occasionally while cooking. Turn shish kebabs for even cooking. Fish is ready when opaque and flakes easily with a fork. Serve with rice and grilled corn-on-the-cob. Serves 6-8.

Pesto Basting Sauce

Ingredients:
- ½ cup (125 ml) **olive oil**
- ½ cup (125 ml) **parsley** leaves
- ¼ cup (60 ml) **lemon juice**
- 2 **cloves garlic**
- 1 tsp (5 ml) dried **basil**

Method:
Place all ingredients in a blender or food processor and process until garlic and parsley are finely chopped. Pour into bowl and baste.

SEAFOOD

Individual Oyster Pies 65

Microwaved
Crab Fettuccine 42

Clam Griddle Cakes
with Cran-Applesauce 21

Smoked
Oyster Log71

New England Clam Chowder 153

Mushroom & Zucchini Halibut Packages

Ingredients:

- 4 oz (115 g) **mushrooms**, sliced
- 2 sprigs fresh **tarragon**, tops reserved and leaves finely chopped OR 2 tsp (10 ml) dried
- 1 tsp (5 ml) **lemon juice**
- **Salt** and **pepper** to taste
- 2 Tbsp (30 ml) **butter**, melted OR **olive oil**
- 2 **halibut** steaks, 1 inch (2.5 cm) thick (7 oz / 200 g ea)
- 1 medium **zucchini**, sliced

Method:

Place mushrooms, half of the chopped tarragon, lemon juice, salt and pepper in a small bowl; stir together. Preheat oven to 375°F (190°C). Cut two pieces of heavy-duty foil into 12 inch x 18 inch (30-46 cm) squares and brush lightly with melted butter or olive oil. Place mushroom mixture over half the foil and place a steak on top and season with salt and pepper. Arrange zucchini slices over fish. Sprinkle with remaining fresh or dried tarragon. Fold foil over fish and fold in a ½ inch (1.5 cm) edge of foil and crimp to seal. Place packages on a baking sheet in oven and bake for 12-15 minutes. Halibut should be opaque and flake easily when fork-tested. Place each package on plate and serve, pinching package tops open at the table. Serves 2.

Broiled Halibut Almondine

Ingredients:

Salt to taste
2 lbs (1 kg) halibut fillets OR steaks
6 Tbsp (90 ml) butter OR margarine, melted and divided
¼ cup (60 ml) Parmesan cheese, grated, divided
¼ lb (115 g) mushrooms, sliced
¼ cup (60 ml) almonds, toasted, halved
2 tomatoes (optional)
Few parsley sprigs (optional)

Method:

Sprinkle salt on both sides of fish. Brush with 2 Tbsp (30 ml) butter and sprinkle with half of the Parmesan cheese. Lightly coat broiler pan with non-stick cooking spray. Place fillets on pan and broil 4 inches (10 cm) from heat source for about 7 minutes on the first side, turn and brush second side with 2 Tbsp (30 ml) butter and sprinkle with remaining cheese, broil for an additional 5-6 minutes or until fish is opaque and flakes when fork-tested. While fish is cooking, sauté mushrooms in remaining butter. Arrange fish on a warmed serving platter and circle with almonds and mushrooms. Garnish with quartered tomatoes and parsley sprigs.

Vegetarian: Another word for a poor fisherman!

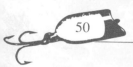

Sweet and Sour Halibut

Ingredients:
- 2 Tbsp (30 ml) salad **oil**
- 1 medium **onion**, chopped
- 1 green **pepper**, cut into strips
- 1 Tbsp (15 ml) **soy sauce**
- ¼ cup (60 ml) **vinegar**
- 1 can (2 ½ cups / 625 ml) **pineapple** tidbits, drained, reserved
- 2 Tbsp (30 ml) **corn starch**
- 1 tsp (5 ml) ground **ginger**
- 1 Tbsp (15 ml) **brown sugar**
- 2 lbs (1 kg) **halibut** steaks
- **Salt** and **pepper** to taste

Method:

Preheat oven to 350°F (180°C). Heat oil in skillet, sauté onion and green pepper until onion is translucent. In a cup combine all liquids with corn starch, ginger and sugar. Add to pan with pineapple. Cook, stirring until blended and thickened. Arrange steaks in a shallow lightly greased baking dish. Season with salt and pepper. Pour sauce over top. Bake for 20-25 minutes. Steaks should be opaque and flake when fork-tested.

Garlic Parmesan Halibut

Ingredients:
- 1 cup (250 ml) **water**
- **Salt** to taste
- 4 ½ tsp (22 ml) **lemon juice**
- 1 lb (454 g) **halibut** fillets, cut into bite size pieces
- 1 **clove garlic**, minced
- 1 tsp (5 ml) **lemon** rind, grated
- **Parsley**, chopped
- ½-1 cup (125-250 ml) **mushrooms**, sliced
- 2 Tbsp (30 ml) **margarine**
- **Parmesan cheese**

Method:

Put water, salt and lemon juice in a saucepan, add fish. Cover and simmer, turning once, until fish flakes easily when fork-tested, about 5 minutes. Drain. In heavy fry pan, sauté garlic, lemon rind, parsley, and mushrooms in butter. Place cooked fish on a serving platter and pour mushroom mixture over the top. Sprinkle with cheese.

Halibut Croquettes

Ingredients:
- 1 cup (250 ml) **halibut**, cold, cooked
- ½ cup (125 ml) **bread crumbs**, fresh, cubed
- ½ tsp (2 ml) **onion**, chopped
- 1 **egg yolk**
- 2 Tbsp (30 ml) **milk**
- ½ tsp (2 ml) **parsley**, chopped
- ½ tsp (2 ml) **salt**
- Dash red **pepper**
- **Flour** for dusting
- 1 **egg + egg white**
- **Bread crumbs**, dried, crushed fine
- **Oil** for frying

Method:

In a medium size glass bowl, mix together fish, breadcrumbs, onion, egg yolk, milk, parsley, salt and red pepper. Chill for one hour for easier handling. Using ¼-½ cup (60-125 ml) and with floured hands, shape mixture into croquettes. Whisk together the egg and remaining egg white. Dip croquette into egg mixture then roll into dried crumbs. In a large heavy fry pan heat oil until hot, fry croquettes, turning once, until crispy and golden brown, about 4-5 minutes per side. Serve with Tartar Sauce, recipe on page 12.

Oven-fried Halibut

Ingredients:
- 1 Tbsp (15 ml) **butter**
- 1 Tbsp (15 ml) **oil**
- ½ cup (125 ml) **Westcoaster Shakin' Bake Mix**, see recipe on page 114
- ⅓ cup (80 ml) **milk**
- 2 lbs (1 kg) **halibut** fillets, cut into serving-size pieces

Method:

In glass baking dish, heat butter and oil in oven until butter melts. Remove from oven. Combine Seafood coating mix and place on a flat dinner-size plate. Pour milk onto a pie plate. Dip fish into milk, into coating mix, then turn fish into butter-oil mixture, and return to oven. Bake in a 425°F (220°C) oven for approximately 10-12 minutes or until fish is opaque and flakes when fork-tested.

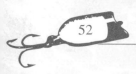

Port Gamble Fish Salad

Ingredients:
- 3 lbs (1.5 kg) fresh OR frozen **halibut** fillets
- 2 cups (500 ml) **mayonnaise**
- ⅓ cup (80 ml) **lemon juice**
- 1 Tbsp (15 ml) **onion**, grated
- 2 tsp (10 ml) **salt**
- ½ tsp (2 ml) **pepper**
- 1 tsp (5 ml) **curry powder**
- 1 tsp (5 ml) **Worcestershire sauce**
- ⅛ tsp (.5 ml) **Tabasco**
- 2 envelopes (2 Tbsp/30 ml) unflavored **gelatin**
- 1 cup (250 ml) liquid (fish cooking **liquid** + **water**)
- ½ cup (125 ml) **parsley**, chopped
- **Shrimp**, cooked, chilled (optional)

Method:

If you are using frozen fish, thaw until fillets come apart easily. Rinse fish under cold running water. Put a rack in a large roaster pan. Lay a large sheet of heavy-duty aluminum foil on rack. Lay the pieces of fish on the foil and turn up edges so any liquid from fish is saved. Pour ½ inch (1.5 cm) of boiling water into the pan. Do not let water touch fish, it is to steam. Cover pan tightly and simmer 10 minutes per inch (2.5 cm) of thickness. Fish should be opaque and flake easily when tested with a fork. When done lift fish out and into a bowl. Set aside to cool. Drain any liquid from the foil into a measuring cup and add water, if necessary, to make 1 cup (250 ml). Chill.

Flake the cooled fish, removing any bones, skin or dark meat. In a bowl combine mayonnaise, lemon juice, onion, salt, pepper, curry powder, Worcestershire sauce and Tabasco. Add fish and beat on medium speed of mixer until very smooth. In a small saucepan sprinkle gelatin over 1 cup (250 ml) of the cold cooking liquid for 5 minutes. Over low heat, heat and stir until gelatin is dissolved but do not let it boil. Slowly pour, in a thin stream, into fish mixture beating constantly. Stir in parsley. Pour into a 2 qt (2 l) mold with a tube in the center. Chill for several hours until very firm. Unmold onto a bed of watercress and fill center with chilled shrimp if desired. Serves 8.

Mixed Seafood

Seafood of all types mix so well together without overpowering each other. The varied colors and textures make an eye-appealing meal that anyone will enjoy. Try our Washington Mixed Seafood Grill at your next outdoor get-together.

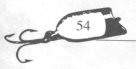

Seashore Salad

Ingredients:
- 1 head iceberg **lettuce**
- 1 box cherry **tomatoes**
- 1 large **carrot**
- 1 stalk **celery**
- 5 **radishes**
- 1 head **cauliflower**
- 1 **cucumber**
- 1 cup (250 ml) alfalfa **sprouts**
- 1 can (8 oz / 227 ml) **salmon**
- 1 can (8 oz / 227 ml) **crab**
- 1 can (8 oz / 227 ml) **tuna**
- 1 can (8 oz / 227 ml) **shrimp**
- Favorite **dressing**

Method:
Wash and trim vegetables. Cut into bite-size pieces. Drain and remove any bones and skin from salmon, flake into large chunks. Check canned crab for shells and flake. Flake and drain tuna. Separate shrimp. Place all ingredients in a large bowl and toss with your favorite dressing.

Seafood Cocktail

Ingredients:
- 6 oz (170 ml) cooked **salmon**
- 6 oz (170 ml) cooked **halibut** OR any firm, white fish
- 6 oz (170 ml) cooked **shrimp**, shelled and deveined
- ½ cup (125 ml) **celery**, diced
- **Salt** to taste
- 1 **lemon**, juice only
- ½ **cucumber**, diced
- 1 bottle (14 oz / 398 ml) **ketchup**
- 2 tsp (10 ml) **horseradish**
- 2 tsp (10 ml) **Worcestershire**
- 2 tsp (10 ml) minced green **pepper**
- 2 tsp (10 ml) **lemon juice**

Method:
In a large bowl, mix first 7 ingredients together and chill. For sauce, mix together ketchup, horseradish, Worcestershire sauce, green pepper and 2 tsp (10 ml) lemon juice. Chill. When ready to serve, arrange fish mixture on lettuce leaves and top with sauce.

Mixed Washington Seafood Grill

Ingredients:

24 small **clams**
1 lb (454 g) large fresh
  shrimp
⅓ cup (80 ml) olive OR
  salad **oil**
¾ tsp (4 ml) **savory**
¾ tsp (4 ml) **chervil**
¾ tsp (4 ml) **salt**
Vegetable **cooking spray**
1 **halibut** steak, cut 1 inch
  (2.5 cm) thick
  (about 2 lbs/1 kg)
Watercress sprigs for
  garnish

Method:

Scrub clams under running water with a stiff brush. Cut legs from shrimp with kitchen shears. Devein shrimp by inserting tip of kitchen shears under shell; cut along back through tail to remove vein, leaving shell on shrimp. Rinse shrimp under running cold water. Mix olive oil, savory, chervil and salt in a large mixing bowl. Add shrimp to oil mixture and stir until coated. Place barbecue grill over medium high heat, when ready to cook, spray or brush with vegetable oil. Place shrimp and halibut on grill; brush halibut with remaining marinade. Cover, cook shrimp, turning once and basting, 4-6 minutes or until the shells turn pink and the meat turns a snowy white. Cook halibut 8-10 minutes, turning once and basting, or until fish is opaque and flakes easily with a fork. Place clams on grill with deep shell side down to hold juices. Cook until shells open about 3-6 minutes. Discard any shells that do not open. Arrange seafood on a large warm platter. Garnish with watercress sprigs. Serve with Sweet Tomato-Chili Sauce, see recipe on page 10.

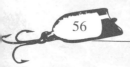

Shrimp, Crab & Mushroom Rolls

Ingredients:

1 can (10 oz/284 ml) **shrimp**
1 can (10 oz/284 ml) **crab**
¼ cup (60 ml) **butter**
2 cups (500 ml) fresh **mushrooms**, sliced
¼ cup (60 ml) **flour**
2 cups (500 ml) chicken OR fish **stock**
1 cup (250 ml) heavy **cream**
3 Tbsp (45 ml) dry **sherry**
2 **egg** yolks
1 tsp (5 ml) **salt**
¼ tsp (1 ml) **pepper**
⅛ tsp (.5 ml) **nutmeg**
1 Tbsp (15 ml) **butter**
¼ cup (60 ml) **onion**, finely, chopped
Pinch **thyme** leaf
12 thin **pancakes** (approx. 6 inches/15 cm in diameter)
2 Tbsp (30 ml) Swiss **cheese**, grated

Method:

Drain shrimp and crab. Break into bowl. Heat ¼ cup (60 ml) butter in heavy saucepan. Add mushrooms and cook gently for 3 minutes. Lift out mushrooms with slotted spoon and add to shrimp and crab. Sprinkle flour into butter remaining in pan, cook one minute, stirring constantly. Remove from heat. Add chicken or fish stock all at once. Return to moderate heat and bring to a boil, stirring constantly, until smooth and thick.

Beat cream, sherry, egg yolks, salt, pepper and nutmeg together with a fork. Stir into hot mixture gradually. Cook, stirring constantly, until boiling. Remove from heat. Measure out 1 cup (250 ml) of mixture and combine with crab, shrimp and mushrooms. Heat 1 Tbsp (15 ml) butter in small skillet. Add onion and cook gently for 3 minutes. Add to remaining sauce with thyme. Pre-heat oven to 350°F (180°C). Butter a baking dish (12 inch x 8 inch x 2 inch /30 x 21 x 5 cm). Top 12 pancakes with part of shrimp/crab/mushroom mixture and roll each one up. Place in baking dish, seam side down. Pour sauce over top and sprinkle with cheese. Bake 350°F (180°C) about 20 minutes or until sauce is bubbling. Serve immediately.

Bay Seafood Salad with Cilantro

Ingredients:
½ cup (125 ml) **beer** OR
dry white **wine**
1 **clove garlic**, sliced in half
1 **bay leaf**
4 fresh **mussels** with
shells, debearded and
scrubbed
4 fresh large **shrimp**,
peeled and deveined
4 fresh **scallops**, shucked
and rinsed
1 Tbsp (15 ml) cooking
liquid
1 Tbsp (15 ml) **lemon juice**
1 tsp (5 ml) Dijon-style
mustard
1 tsp (5 ml) **olive oil**
½ tsp (2 ml) ground **cumin**
½ tsp (2 ml) jalapeño
pepper, seeded and
chopped
¼ tsp (1 ml) **garlic**, finely
chopped
1 Tbsp (15 ml) fresh
cilantro, chopped
Salt and **pepper** to taste
2 cups (500 ml) mixed
salad greens

Method:
In a large saucepan over
medium heat bring beer, sliced
garlic, and bay leaf to a boil.
Add seafood, cover and simmer
until mussels open, about
5 minutes. Remove mussels
from saucepan and scoop out
meat from shells, set aside.
Remove shrimp when white,
about 2 minutes. Cook scallops
until opaque and firm, about
3 minutes, remove. Reserve
1 Tbsp (15 ml) cooking liquid.
Refrigerate all until ready to
serve.

To make dressing: Mix the
reserved cooking liquid with
lemon juice, mustard, oil,
cumin, jalapeño pepper,
chopped garlic, cilantro, salt
and pepper. Mix with seafood
and let stand in refrigerator for
at least 1 hour. Toss seafood
and serve on salad greens.

Mussels

Mussels are a familiar sight to Westcoasters. Mussels abound on rocky shores and on pilings. However, you should not eat mussels growing on pilings as they may be contaminated by the chemicals used to preserve the wood. The bluish-black clusters of mussels are easily obtained at low-tide where they attach themselves to rock exposed to the surf with tough hair-like "byssus" or beard. Pry mussels off rocks with a screwdriver. Don't use any mussels if the shell is open or damaged or fails to close tightly when tapped.

If you are preparing and eating your mussels on the beach, place them in a bucket of fresh sea water letting them stand so they clean themselves of sand. If taking home, cover the mussels with damp cloths or seaweed and keep in a cool place until ready to clean. To clean, place them in a bucket of fresh water with ½ cup (125 ml) of salt added. Let them stand for about 20 minutes then drain. Make sure mussel shells are tightly closed or that they do close when lightly tapped.

Prepare mussels for cooking by scraping off any barnacles. Scrub with a stiff brush under running water to remove all grit. Cut off the beard by pulling out any threads at the hinge. Mussels are ready to cook in any of the fine recipes in this book. The simplest cooking method is to put them in a large pan with 1 inch (2.5 cm) of water. Cover and steam for about 5-10 minutes or until shells open. Throw away any shells that don't open! Or grill them over a hot grate with the larger side of the shell down holding the juice. Shells will open when cooked, about 2-6 minutes. Discard any that do not open. You can store mussels in the refrigerator for up to 2 days by arranging them in a shallow dish and covering with a damp tea towel. Before cooking, discard any dead mussels.

CAUTION: From May 1 through October mussels may be dangerous to eat on the Pacific coast. Pay heed to quarantine posting.

Pasta with Mussel Sauce

Ingredients:
24 large **mussels**
2 Tbsp (30 ml) salad **oil**
1 medium **onion**, chopped
1 **clove garlic**, crushed
1 can (16 oz/455 ml) **tomatoes**, undrained
1 can (6 oz/170 ml) **tomato paste**
3 Tbsp (45 ml) **parsley**, chopped
2 Tbsp (30 ml) dry white **wine** OR **apple juice**
1 tsp (5 ml) **sugar**
¼ tsp (1 ml) red **pepper**, crushed
Salt to taste
1 pkg (16 oz/454 g) **linguine**

Method:
Clean mussels as described on page 59. Place mussels in a large saucepan or Dutch oven, with 1 inch (2.5 cm) of water and heat to boiling. Reduce heat to medium-low; cover and cook 5-10 minutes or until shells are open. Discard shells of any mussels that do not open. Rinse any remaining sand from mussels with cooking broth. Remove meat from shell and chop, set aside. Let sand settle in the cooking broth, then remove ¾ cup (175 ml) of broth. Heat a light-flavored oil in a 4 qt (4 l) saucepan and cook onion and garlic until tender. Add reserved cooking broth, tomatoes and juice, tomato paste, parsley, wine, sugar, red pepper and salt to taste. Heat to boiling, stirring occasionally to break up tomatoes. Reduce heat, cover pan and simmer 15 minutes, stirring often. Cook linguine as package directs. To serve, heat mussels through in sauce and serve over hot linguine. Serves 6.

Remember this?
"Cockles and Mussels in Dublin's fair city, where the girls are so pretty…crying Cockles and Mussels alive , alive O!"

Traditional French Mussels

Ingredients:
- 2 lbs (1 kg) fresh **mussels**
- 1 cup (250 ml) **onion**, finely chopped
- ½ cup (125 ml) **celery**, finely chopped
- 2 Tbsp (30 ml) **garlic**, finely chopped
- 2 Tbsp (30 ml) fresh **thyme**, chopped
- ¼ cup (60 ml) fresh **parsley**, chopped
- 2 Tbsp (30 ml) fresh **basil**, chopped
- 2 cups (500 ml) fruity white **wine**
- **Pepper** to taste
- ¼ cup (60 ml) **butter**

Method:

Clean mussels as described on page 59. Place in a large pot with onions, celery, garlic, thyme, 2 Tbsp (30 ml) of the parsley, basil, and wine. Cover, bring to a boil. Shake pan occasionally to distribute juices and to help mussels open, about 5-10 minutes. Remove mussels with a slotted spoon and set aside. Discard any that do not open. Simmer sauce for 2 minutes, adding pepper if needed. Add butter to sauce and gently stir until melted. Pour into serving bowls, add mussels and sprinkle with remaining parsley. Serve with french fries and salad for a main meal. Serves 4.

The fisherman's marriage proposal: "Wanted: Winsome widow woman wallowing in wealth. I will grant you scads of wishes, say you caught the biggest fishes, even help you with the dishes. You will be my cuddle bunny, I will even call you honey..."

Mussels on the Half Shell

Ingredients:

36 large **mussels**
½ cup (125 ml) **butter** OR
   margarine
1 small **onion**, chopped
3 cups (750 ml) soft **bread
   crumbs**
¼ tsp (1 ml) freshly
   ground **pepper**
¼ tsp (1 ml) **thyme** leaves
¼ tsp (1 ml) **marjoram**
   leaves
¼ cup (60 ml) **pine nuts**
Topping (recipe follows)

Method:

Clean mussels as described on page 59. Steam mussels by placing them in a large pot containing 1 inch (2.5 cm) of water. Bring to a boil. Tightly cover pot and steam until shells open, about 5 minutes. Remove mussels from pot, discard any mussels that do not open, remove meat from shells. Reserve ¼ cup (60 ml) of cooking broth and the shells. Chop meat and set aside. Preheat oven to 350°F (180°C). Melt butter in a fry pan over medium heat. Add onion to pan juices and cook until soft.

Remove onions to a bowl and add meat, bread crumbs, pepper, thyme, marjoram, and reserved broth. Mix thoroughly. Place nuts in a single layer in a pan and broil in oven for about 6 minutes, stirring occasionally until golden brown. Prepare topping. Spoon mussel mixture into 18 of the largest half shells. Sprinkle with nuts and topping. Place stuffed shells in a shallow baking dish surrounded by crumbled tin foil or 1 inch (2.5 cm) of rock salt. Bake in a 425°F (220°C) oven for 5-10 minutes or until golden brown. These make an excellent appetizer.

Topping

Ingredients:

½ cup (125 ml) **butter** OR
   margarine, melted
1 cup (250 ml) **cracker
   crumbs**, finely crushed
¼ cup (60 ml) **parsley**,
   chopped

Method:

In a small bowl, mix ingredients until well blended.

Herb Mussels

Ingredients:
  2 Tbsp (30 ml) vegetable
  oil
  6 **shallots**, chopped
  2 **cloves garlic**, chopped
  1 cup (250 ml) coconut
  milk
  2 Tbsp (30 ml) **lime juice**
  1 tsp (5 ml) **lime rind**,
  grated
  1 tsp (5 ml) Thai **chili
  sauce** OR **sambal oelek**
  2 lbs (1 kg) fresh **mussels**
  2 Tbsp (30 ml) fresh **mint**
  OR **coriander**, chopped
  2 Tbsp (30 ml) fresh **basil**,
  chopped

Method:
  Clean mussels as described on page 59. In saucepan heat oil over medium heat. Add shallots and garlic; sauté only until soft. Stir in coconut milk, lime juice, rind and chili sauce. Bring to boil, reduce heat to medium. Cook for 2 minutes. Add mussels. Return to boil. Cover pan, steam about 4-6 minutes or until mussels open. Remove mussels and set aside. Discard any that do not open. To sauce, add mint or coriander and basil, simmer 1 minute. Pour into 4 bowls, add mussels. Serves 4.

The fisherman's divine hope: Then God commanded, Let the water be filled with many kinds of living beings... And God was pleased with what he saw. He blessed them all and told the creatures that live in the water to reproduce and fill the sea... Then God said, And now we will make man; they will have power over the fish....

(Taken from Genesis 1:20-28.)

Oysters

Westcoasters can enjoy both the native Olympia oyster and the large Pacific oyster. Live oysters are best kept in the shell, covered with damp cloths, in the refrigerator for no more than 24 hours. Shuck (pry open) oysters just before serving. Keep on ice throughout the shucking process. Once oysters are shucked, you should eat them the same day. For longer storage, shucked oysters may be frozen in an airtight container for up to 4 months. Do not attempt to eat oysters from shells that do not close when touched as this means the oyster is dead and should not be eaten. The "R" months' rule, only eat oysters in which the months have an "R" in them is a good rule to follow.

To clean oysters for eating, scrub the shells under cold running water with a stiff brush. Discard open shells as mentioned previously. When all are cleaned, place the oysters, cupped side down on a hard surface. Insert a strong, blunt knife between the shells near the hinge and with a twisting motion pry the shells apart. Following the contour of the shell, move knife around to cut the muscle that holds the two shells together. It is a good idea to wear a glove, on the hand holding the oyster, while performing this operation in case the knife slips. Save the liquid (liquor) inside as this is often used in recipes along with the meat.

Oysters may also be steamed open. Rinse and scrub oysters as above. Place oysters in a kettle with a small amount of water, not more than ½ cup (125 ml) for 2 dozen medium-sized oysters. Steam for 5-10 minutes, or until shells are open. Carefully lift oysters out of pan so you don't spill the liquor. Or, to grill, scrub shells as above, heat grill until very hot. Place oysters with larger side of shell directly on grill rack, cook for about 5-8 minutes or until shells open. Discard any that do not open.

Shucked oysters should not be overcooked as they become tough. Use moderate heat and cook just until they are plump and edges begin to curl, anywhere from 2-5 minutes. Or, some like them not cooked at all but eaten fresh right from the shell.

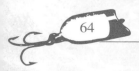

Oriental Shrimp
Stir-fry 121

SEAFOOD

BYOF* Cioppino
(Soup) Party 152

Thai Shrimp
with Sesame Noodles 126

Cocktail
Seafood
Salad 41

Individual Oyster Pies

Ingredients:
24 **oysters**, shucked OR
  1 jar (16 oz / 500 g),
  drained and reserve
  liquid
½ tsp (2 ml) **salt** or to taste
Pinch of **tarragon**
Pinch of cayenne **pepper**
Pinch of black **pepper**
2 tsp (10 ml)
  Worcestershire sauce
½ cup (125 ml) **onion**,
  chopped
2 **carrots**, sliced
4 medium **potatoes**, diced
1 cup (250 ml) Cheddar
  cheese, grated
Milk
Pastry

Method:
Cut oysters into small pieces (kitchen scissors work well for this) and mix with salt, tarragon, cayenne pepper, black pepper, and Worcestershire sauce. Set aside. In individual casserole dishes, layer onions, then carrots and, lastly, potatoes. Cover with a layer of oysters and cheese. Repeat. Mix 2 Tbsp (30 ml) milk and 2 Tbsp (30 ml) liquid, reserved from oysters, for each casserole. Pour over each casserole. Cover with pastry that has been well slashed to allow steam to escape. Bake in 400°F (200°C) oven until vegetables are tender and crust is golden brown, approximately 20 minutes.

Seafood is the perfect food choice for health-conscious individuals. It's proven to be an excellent source of protein and is low in calories, fat and cholesterol. It's also low in sodium and a great source of vitamins and minerals.

Scalloped Oyster Pie

Ingredients:
- ½ cup (125 ml) **butter** OR **margarine**, melted, divided
- 3 **scallions**, white and light green parts only, finely chopped
- 2 cups (500 ml) **cracker crumbs**, medium-coarse
- 3 cups (750 ml) fresh shucked **oysters**, drained, reserve liquid (about 3 dozen)
- **Pepper** to taste
- ½ cup (125 ml) light **cream**
- **Salt** to taste
- ¼ tsp (1 ml) **Worcestershire sauce**
- Dash of **Tabasco**

Method:

Melt butter over medium heat in cast iron fry pan. Cook scallions until soft, about 3 minutes. Add cracker crumbs and toss with a fork. Grease a shiny 9 inch (23 cm) baking pan. Evenly spread ⅓ of the crumb mixture on the bottom. Arrange half the oysters on the crumbs and sprinkle with pepper. Sprinkle on another ⅓ of the crumbs, the remaining oysters and sprinkle again with pepper. (Make layers no more than two oysters deep so they will remain big and fluffy.) Combine reserved liquid from oysters and cream to make 1 cup (250 ml). Stir in salt, Worcestershire sauce and Tabasco. Pour sauce over oysters and sprinkle with remaining crumbs. Bake in a 350°F (180°C) oven for 30-40 minutes or until puffy and moist with a crunchy top. Serves 4.

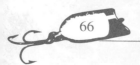

Spicy Fried Oysters

Contributed by Marg Shama, Victoria, B.C., Canada

Ingredients:
- 12 **Oysters**, shucked, drained, rinsed
- **Flour** mixture (see below)
- **Oil**

Flour Mixture:

- 1 cup (250 ml) whole wheat **flour**
- 1 tsp (5 ml) **garam masala**
- 1 tsp (5 ml) chili OR cayenne **pepper**
- **Salt** to taste

Method:

In large bowl, combine flour, garam masala, chili pepper and salt. Dredge oysters in flour mixture. In a cast iron fry pan heat oil until hot. Fry oysters in two batches for approximately 75 seconds on first side and 45 seconds on second side. Serve immediately.

Oyster Wraps

Ingredients:
- 18 small to medium fresh shucked **oysters**
- 9 strips lean **bacon**
- ¼ cup (60 ml) **Parmesan cheese**

Method:

Drain oysters on a paper towel and pat dry. Cut strips of bacon in half; wrap around each oyster securing with a toothpick. Broil under a low-heat broiler, cook until oysters are firm and bacon is crisp, turning wraps to ensure even cooking, about 8-10 minutes. When done, sprinkle with Parmesan cheese, serve.

Snappy Oyster Appetizers

Ingredients:
24 small, fresh shucked
oysters, drained, but
liquid reserved
¼ cup (60 ml) **rice vinegar**
2 Tbsp (30 ml) **soy sauce**
½ cup (125 ml) **cashews**,
finely ground
½ cup (125 ml)
mayonnaise
1 tsp (5 ml) **lemon juice**
1 Tbsp (15 ml) **soy sauce**
½ tsp (2 ml) **curry powder**
1-2 drops **Tabasco sauce**
2 slices **bacon**, cut in 1 inch
(2.5 cm) pieces

Method:
Place oysters in a medium-size bowl. Pour reserved liquid from oysters, vinegar, and 2 Tbsp (30 ml) soy sauce over oysters, cover and marinade for at least 30 minutes in the refrigerator. Drain. Roll oysters in the ground cashews. Line a shallow baking dish with lightly buttered foil. Lay oysters in a single layer, slightly apart in pan. Blend mayonnaise, lemon juice, 1 Tbsp (15 ml) soy sauce, curry powder and Tabasco. Place 1 Tbsp (15 ml) of sauce on each oyster. Place a piece of bacon on top and broil 3 inches (7.5 cm) from heat source for 5 minutes or until oysters start to curl at the edges and bacon sizzles. Serve on crackers or toast rounds.

When buying your fish fresh, be sure to check the fish for signs of freshness. Fillets and steaks should have moist, firm flesh, and whole fish should have clear eyes and bright metallic markings.

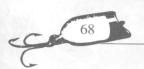

Seashore Oyster Omelet

Ingredients:
   2 strips **bacon**, chopped
      OR 2 Tbsp (30 ml) **bacon
      drippings**
   2 cups (500 ml) whole
      fresh shucked small
      oysters OR large fresh
      shucked **oysters**,
      quartered
   ½ cup (125 ml) oyster
      liquor, reserved from jar
      OR fresh liquor
   ¼ cup (60 ml) **scallions** OR
      green **onion**s, chopped
   6 **eggs**, beaten
   1 can whole kernel **corn**,
      drained
   Salt and **pepper** to taste
   Paprika to taste
   Italian **seasonings** to taste

Method:
   In an 8 inch (21 cm) heavy
skillet, fry bacon until crisp or
heat drippings. Add oysters
and oyster liquor; simmer over
medium heat until liquor is
reduced and oysters curl at the
edges, about 3-4 minutes. Add
scallions, pour beaten eggs over
oysters. Add corn over all.
Season to taste with salt,
pepper and seasonings of your
choice. If cooking on the beach
over a bonfire, cover pan and
cook slowly until eggs are firm,
about 15 minutes, tilting pan a
couple of times to allow
uncooked egg to run to the
bottom of pan. If cooking in the
oven; bake, uncovered at 300°F
(150°C) for about 15 minutes, or
until knife inserted in the center
comes out clean. Serve with
Sweet Tomato-Chili Sauce, see
recipe on page 10.

Long Island Oyster Toast

Ingredients:

4-6 slices firm, white **bread**
½ cup (125 ml) **butter**
2 pts (1 l) fresh shucked
   oysters, reserve liquid
2 Tbsp (30 ml) **catsup**
1 Tbsp (15 ml)
   Worcestershire sauce
1 Tbsp (15 ml) **lemon juice**
Salt and **pepper** to taste
Parsley, chopped

Method:

Arrange bread on a rack (so heat can circulate). Place in a 300°F (150°C) oven for 20-25 minutes or until bread is dry and lightly brown. Spread with some butter, keep warm. Melt remaining butter in a large fry pan over medium heat; add oysters and liquid, catsup, Worcestershire sauce, and lemon juice. Cook until oysters are plump and edges curled, about 3-4 minutes. Turn over several times during cooking. Using a slotted spoon place oysters evenly on toast. Keep warm. Boil juice remaining in the fry pan until reduced to ½ cup (125 ml). Spoon juice over oysters and season with salt and pepper, topped with parsley. Serve while hot. Serves 4-6.

Stranger than fiction:

The Sharpshooter Fish. Many fish like to eat insects. One of these is the archer fish. Other fish have to catch insects in their mouths. Not the archer. He can just shoot them down. The archer points his head at a bug and spits. The drop of water shot from the archer's mouth hits the insect so hard it is knocked out.

Very Good Oyster Fritters

Ingredients:
2 jars (12 oz/341 ml ea)
   oysters
1 cup (250 ml) **flour**
Salt to taste
Dash cayenne **pepper**
⅔ cup (150 ml) **water**
2 Tbsp (30 ml) **oil** OR
   melted **fat**
1 **egg yolk**, beaten
1 **egg white**, stiffly beaten

Method:
Drain oysters, place on paper towel to absorb excess moisture. Combine dry ingredients. Combine water, fat and egg yolk; gradually add to flour mixture, stirring until blended. Do not over mix. Let stand 1 hour. Fold egg white into batter. Heat fat in deep-fryer or deep heavy saucepan, to 375°F (190°C). Dip oysters into batter and fry for 3-4 minutes or until golden brown. Drain on paper towel. Serve with Remoulade Sauce on page 12.

Smoked Oyster Log

Contributed by Peggy Crawford, Victoria, B.C., Canada

Ingredients:
1 pkg (8 oz/225 g) **cream
   cheese**, softened
1 ½ Tbsp (22 ml) **mayonnaise**
1 tsp (5 ml) **Worcestershire
   sauce**
1 tsp (5 ml) **soy sauce**
Dash **garlic powder**
Dash **onion powder**
Salt and **pepper** to taste
Few drops **Tabasco sauce**
1 can smoked **oysters**,
   drained and chopped
Parsley, chopped

Method:
In a small bowl, blend together cheese, mayonnaise, Worcestershire sauce, soy sauce, garlic and onion powders, salt, pepper and Tabasco. Spread mixture onto waxed paper, approximately ¼ inch (.5 cm) thick, 6" x 12" (15 x 30 cm) spread with chopped oysters. Place a sheet of wax paper on top and refrigerate for 30-60 minutes. Remove and roll as for jelly-roll. Cover roll with chopped parsley. Serve with your favorite crackers.

Salmon

Salmon! The king of Northwest Coast fish. As nutritious as it is delicious. Do we need to say more?

Salmon Basics

Contributed by Janice Bowden, Chemainus, B.C., Canada

The eyes of a fresh fish should look bright and clear, the gills should be reddish, the skin moist with shiny, tightly-adhered scales. The touch should give slightly and spring back into shape when gently pressed. A fresh fish should have a seaweedy odor but never smell fishy or offensive.

Gut and wash fish. It is best to leave head on but if you want to remove head, cut at base and around gill area removing gills. If the fish has already been gutted, wash with cold water, removing any darkened or yellow areas along edges. Your nose is a valuable asset. If the edges smell rancid, trim off about a ¼ inch (.5 cm) so the flesh is a pink to red color. If it has a bit of freezer burn, trim and sprinkle liberally with garlic. Then lay the fish on a suitable baking sheet or glass dish. Cover with foil, making it fit around the edges of pan firmly.

Bake at 425°F (220°C) for 30-60 minutes depending on size of fish. It's approximately 10 minutes per inch (2.5 cm) at thickest part of fresh or fully thawed fish including stuffing if used. If partially thawed, bake 12-15 minutes per inch (2.5 cm) or if solidly frozen, bake 20 minutes per inch (2.5 cm). And, if salmon is foil-wrapped or heavily sauced add 5 minutes to total cooking time. Do not overcook fish, salmon is naturally tender. To check if done, remove from oven, poke a fork in the thickest part of the fish. Fish should be opaque, moist and flake easily into chunks.

72

Dr. Grove's Smoked Salmon

Ingredients:
  Coarse salt
  Brown sugar

Method:
  In a glass, stainless steel or food-grade plastic, cover salmon fillets with the coarse salt, leaving on for 20-30 minutes in the refrigerator. Rinse off and pat dry. Apply brown sugar, covering fish. Smoke with alder chips for 8-10 hours, using 4-5 trays of alder chips.

Simoon Sound Gourmet Salmon and Mushrooms

Ingredients:
  1 ½ lbs (750 g) **salmon** steaks
  3 Tbsp (45 ml) **butter** OR **margarine**
  2 cups (500 ml) **mushrooms**, sliced
  ½ cup (125 ml) green **onions**, sliced
  Salt and **pepper** to taste
  1 Tbsp (15 ml) fresh **tarragon**, chopped
  3 Tbsp (45 ml) dry white **wine** OR **apple juice**

Method:
  Arrange steaks in a single layer on a greased shallow baking pan. In a small pot, over medium heat, melt butter and sauté mushrooms until just tender. Stir in green onions, salt, pepper and tarragon. Spoon over salmon. Sprinkle with wine. Cover loosely with foil and bake at 425°F (220°C) for 10 minutes per inch (2.5 cm) of thickness. Be sure to add an extra 5 minutes for the foil-wrapping. Fish is cooked when salmon is moist, opaque and flakes when fork-tested. Serve immediately. Serves 4.

Journey's End Baked Salmon with Horseradish

Contributed by Glenna Bendickson, Journey's End, B.C., Canada

Ingredients:
- 2 lbs. (1 kg) **salmon** fillets with skin
- **Salt** and **pepper**
- ¼ cup (60 ml) **whipping cream**, whipped
- ¾ cup (175 ml) fresh white **bread crumbs**
- 3 **shallots**, thinly sliced
- ¾ cup (175 ml) **walnuts**, coarsely chopped
- ¼ cup (60 ml) **mint leaves**, coarsely chopped
- ½ tsp (2 ml) **lemon rind**, freshly grated
- ½ tsp (2 ml) **garlic**, minced
- 1 bottle (6 oz/170 g) **horseradish**
- 2 Tbsp (30 ml) **olive oil**
- 1 cup (250 ml) chicken **stock**
- 2 **shallots**, minced
- 2 Tbsp (30 ml) **cream**
- 1 Tbsp (15 ml) **butter**
- 1 tsp (5 ml) **lemon juice**
- ½ cup (125 ml) **mint** leaves, coarsely chopped

Method:

Preheat oven to 350°F (180°C).

Arrange salmon, skin side down, on a greased baking pan. Sprinkle with salt and pepper. Spread with whipped cream. Chill 15 minutes. Place bread crumbs, shallots, walnuts, ¼ cup (60 ml) mint leaves, lemon rind, garlic, horseradish (squeeze horseradish until almost dry), and olive oil in a bowl and toss together well. Press this crust mixture over the top of the salmon so as to adhere. Bake for 25-30 minutes or until just cooked through. When cooked the salmon should be opaque and flake easily when poked with a fork. Transfer to platter.

While salmon is baking, make the sauce. In a medium saucepan place the stock and shallots. Simmer until reduced to ¼ cup (60 ml). Remove from heat and stir in cream and butter. Whisk in lemon juice so it won't curdle. Add ½ cup (125 ml) mint leaves. Pour sauce around (not over) the salmon on the platter. Serve with roast potatoes and lightly steamed peas.

This unlikely-sounding combination is truly amazing and delicious. A special way we serve salmon to our company here at Journey's End.

Salmon Steaks in Curry Sauce

Contributed by Marg Shama, Victoria, B.C., Canada

Ingredients:

- 1 cup (250 ml) whole wheat **flour**
- 1 tsp (5 ml) **garam masala**
- 1 tsp (5 ml) chili OR cayenne **pepper**
- **Salt** to taste
- 6-8 **salmon** steaks
- **Oil** for frying

Method:

In a large shallow dish, mix dry ingredients together. Dredge the salmon steaks in flour mixture, shake off excess flour and quickly brown both sides in hot oil, set aside.

Sauce

Ingredients:

- 1 large **onion**, finely chopped
- ¾ cup (175 ml) **celery**, chopped
- 2 Tbsp (30 ml) **oil**
- 3 **cloves garlic**, minced
- 1 tsp (5 ml) **salt**
- 1-2 tsp (5 -10 ml) **garam masala**
- 1-2 tsp (5 -10 ml) chili **pepper** OR **cayenne**
- 1-2 tsp (5-10 ml) **turmeric**
- 1-2 tsp (5-10 ml) **curry powder**
- 1 ½ cups (375 ml) **tomato sauce**

Method:

In large saucepan sauté onion and celery in oil. Add garlic. Stir in salt, garam masala, chili pepper or cayenne, turmeric and curry powder. Then mix in tomato sauce. Let mixture cook down, adding water as necessary to keep it soupy. Cook until onions and celery almost disappear. Add fish and let simmer for about 5 minutes or until fish flakes when fork-tested. Serve over rice, but I use it with rotis. Pita bread is a good substitute for the roti.

Teriyaki Salmon

Ingredients:
Teriyaki Marinade,
See recipe on page 16.
Prepare marinade. For
every pound (500 g) of
fish, marinate with
about ⅓ cup (80 ml)
marinade.
Whole or half **salmon**

Method:
Marinate salmon in a glass
dish, cover, refrigerate for about
1 hour. Turn once. Bake in 425°F
(220°C) oven for 10 minutes per
inch (2.5 cm) of thickness or
until fish flakes when fork-
tested. Broil slightly to glaze.

Raisin and Nut Stuffed Salmon

Contributed by Irma Prachneau, Abbotsford, B.C., Canada

Ingredients:
2 Tbsp (30 ml) **butter** OR
margarine
1 cup (250 ml) uncooked
long-grain **rice**
1 **onion**, chopped
¼ cup (60 ml) **almonds** OR
pine nuts, slivered
½ tsp (2 ml) **cumin**
2 cups (500 ml) **boiling
water**
½ cup (125 ml) **raisins**
Salt and **pepper** to taste
3 lbs (1.5 kg) whole or
center-cut **salmon**

Method:
Melt butter in saucepan, then
stir in rice and onion. Cook
over medium heat for 2-3
minutes, stirring occasionally.
Stir in nuts, cumin and boiling
water. Cover and simmer for 20
minutes or until rice is cooked.
Stir in raisins, salt and pepper.
Put salmon on a lightly greased
or oiled sheet of heavy-duty
foil. Stuff salmon loosely with
rice mixture. Seal salmon
tightly in foil and bake in a
425°F (220°C) oven for 10
minutes per inch (2.5 cm) of
thickness plus an extra 5
minutes to penetrate foil.
Salmon is cooked when opaque
and flakes easily when fork-
tested. May be cooked on a
barbecue. Serves 6.

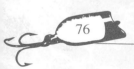

Clo-oose Ginger Salmon

Ingredients:
1 **salmon** fillet (1 lb / 454 g)
Salt and **pepper** to taste
2 Tbsp (30 ml) **lemon juice**
1 Tbsp (15 ml) fresh
   ginger, peeled and
   grated OR 1 ½ tsp (7 ml)
   powdered **ginger**
1 Tbsp (15 ml) vegetable
   oil
Hot **sauce** to taste
¾ cup (175 ml) **sour cream**

Method:
Season salmon on both sides with salt and pepper. In a small bowl, combine lemon juice, ginger, oil and hot sauce. Brush both sides of fillet with sauce. Arrange salmon on a baking dish. Bake at 425°F (220°C) for approximately 10 minutes per inch (2.5 cm) at thickest part or until fish flakes when fork-tested. Remove fish from oven onto a warm serving platter. Pour sour cream into dish salmon has been cooked in and stir over medium heat until warmed through. Serve with sauce over salmon and garnish with parsley sprigs or finely chopped tomatoes.

A priest was walking along the cliffs at Victoria when he came upon two locals pulling another man ashore on the end of a rope. "That's what I like to see." said the priest. "A man helping his fellow man." As he was walking away, one local remarked to the other, "Well, he sure doesn't know the first thing about shark fishing!"

Saucy Grilled Salmon

Ingredients:
- 1 Tbsp (15 ml) **butter**
- 2 medium **shallots**, finely chopped
- ¼ cup (60 ml) **lemon juice**
- 4 tsp. (20 ml) **brown sugar**
- ½ tsp (2 ml) coarse **salt**
- ⅛ tsp (.5 ml) cayenne **pepper**
- 1 Tbsp (15 ml) **ginger**, peeled and finely chopped
- ¼ cup (60 ml) red wine **vinegar**
- 2 Tbsp (30 ml) **soy sauce**
- 2 Tbsp (30 ml) **cilantro**, finely chopped
- 2 lbs (1 kg) **salmon** fillets or four ½ lb (225 g) pieces
- **Lemon** slices
- Fresh **parsley**

Method:
In a small saucepan, melt butter over medium heat. Sauté shallots in the butter only until softened. Add next 7 ingredients and stir well. Remove from heat and mix in cilantro. Rinse fillets under cold running water and blot dry with paper towels. Arrange fish in a glass dish just large enough to hold them. Spoon sauce on both sides of fillets. Cover fish with plastic wrap and let marinate in refrigerator for 30-60 minutes, turning fillets at least once. Preheat grate and oil well using a spray oil bottle, brush or a paper towel, doubled over, and dipped in oil. Spray fillets with oil. Place marinated fillets on hot grate and barbecue about 3 inches (7.5 cm) from heat source for 4-6 minutes each side or until nicely browned, carefully turning over. To test for doneness, poke a fillet with a fork, it should flake into chunks yet be moist when cooked fully. Remove from grill and garnish with lemon and parsley. Discard remaining sauce. Try serving with Mushroom Sauce, see recipe on page 10.

North Sound Grilled Salmon

Ingredients:
- ⅓ cup (80 ml) **butter** OR **margarine**
- ⅔ cup (150 ml) **brown sugar**
- 2 Tbsp (30 ml) **lemon juice**
- 1 Tbsp (15 ml) dry white **wine** OR **apple juice**
- 8 **salmon** fillets (8-10 oz / 225-280 g) each

Method:

Melt butter in a medium-size saucepan over medium heat. Stir in brown sugar until dissolved. Add lemon juice and wine stirring until heated through, about 5 minutes. Baste salmon with marinade. Place salmon in well-greased grill basket. Grill directly over heat source for 4-6 minutes per side or until fish is nicely browned and flakes when fork-tested. Turn over once during cooking and occasionally basting with sauce.

Cajun Grilled Salmon

Ingredients:
- **Cajun Marinade** see recipe on page 17 Prepare marinade. For every pound (500 g) of fish, marinate with about ⅓ cup (80 ml) marinade.
- 8 **salmon** steaks

Method:

Place salmon in glass dish, pour marinade over top, cover with plastic wrap. Let stand in refrigerator for 30 minutes, turning once. To cook, place salmon on well greased hot broiler rack. Broil approximately 4-6 minutes per side, turn and baste with marinade halfway through cooking. Salmon is cooked when nicely browned and fish flakes when fork tested.

Pan Fried Salmon
Steaks with Peppers

Ingredients:
2 Tbsp (30 ml) **olive oil** OR vegetable **oil**, divided

1 large sweet red **pepper**, cut into strips

1 large sweet yellow **pepper**, cut into strips

1 red **onion**, sliced into rings

4 **cloves** of **garlic**, minced

2 Tbsp (30 ml) wine **vinegar**

4 **salmon** steaks

½ tsp (2 ml) **sage**

½ tsp (2 ml) **lemon peel**

½ cup (125 ml) dry white **wine** OR **apple juice** can be substituted for white wine

Salt and **pepper** to taste

Method:
Heat 1 Tbsp (15 ml) olive oil in large fry pan over high heat. Saute red and yellow peppers, onion and garlic until tender. Stir in vinegar. Remove vegetables to oven to keep warm. Add remainder of oil to hot fry pan add salmon steaks, fry just long enough on one side to sear juices in and nicely browned, approximately 1 minute, turn over. Combine spices with wine (or apple juice) and sprinkle over steaks, cover with lid and fry over medium heat for 5-6 minutes or until salmon flakes when tested with a fork. Salmon still should be a little moist looking. Arrange steaks on warmed platter or on individual serving plates and pour warm sauce over the top. Serve immediately. Serves 4.

SEAFOOD

Crunchy Tuna Casserole 170

Tuna in Shells 169

Beans and
Salmon Salad 94

Salmon Crepes Delmonico 98

Halibut Sauté 46

Microwaved Citrus Salmon

Ingredients:

Salt and pepper to taste
1 lb (454 g) salmon fillet
1 Tbsp (15 ml) corn starch
2 Tbsp (30 ml) water
2 Tbsp (30 ml) undiluted
   frozen orange juice
   concentrate
1 Tbsp (15 ml) lemon juice
¼ cup (60 ml) brown sugar
1 orange, sliced (optional)
Parsley, chopped
   (optional)

Method:

Sprinkle salt and pepper on both sides of salmon fillet. In a small bowl, mix corn starch and water to make a paste. Add orange juice concentrate, lemon juice, and brown sugar. Stir until well blended and sugar is dissolved. Pour half of the sauce in a microwave-safe dish. Place salmon in a single layer on top of the sauce and add remaining sauce over the salmon fillet. Cover the dish with plastic wrap, vent to allow steam to escape and cook on HIGH for 7-10 minutes or consult your microwave manual for best results. Salmon is cooked when opaque and flakes easily when tested with a fork yet still moist. Let stand 5 minutes. Take out of microwave and remove plastic wrap carefully. Place salmon on a warmed plate. Pour sauce remaining in the dish over the fillet and garnish with orange slices and parsley.

Tomato Dill Salmon in Microwave

Ingredients:
Salt and pepper to taste
1 lb (454 g) salmon fillet
1 Tbsp (15 ml) fresh dill,
chopped OR
2 tsp (10 ml) dried dill
1 tsp (5 ml) lemon juice
1 Tbsp (15 ml) olive oil
2 Tbsp (30 ml) sun-dried
tomatoes, chopped
2 cloves garlic, finely
chopped
4 sun-dried tomatoes
4 slices lemon

Method:
Sprinkle salt and pepper on both sides of salmon fillet. In a small bowl, mix together dill, lemon juice, oil, tomatoes, and garlic. Rub resulting mixture onto both sides of fillet. Place salmon in a microwave-safe dish, cover with plastic wrap and vent to allow steam to escape. Cook on HIGH for 7-10 minutes. Take out of microwave and carefully remove plastic wrap. Garnish, if desired, with sun-dried tomatoes and lemon slices.

Poached Salmon

Contributed by Alberta Geertsma, Abbotsford, B.C., Canada

Ingredients:
2 lbs (1 kg) salmon fillets
OR steaks
Salt and pepper to taste
2 Tbsp (30 ml) butter
6 thin lemon slices
½ cup (125 ml) white wine
or light grape juice

Method:
Cut salmon into serving-size pieces. Place each piece on a square of heavy-duty foil. Sprinkle each piece of salmon with salt and pepper. Top with a dab of butter, and a slice of lemon. Drizzle wine over the top of each piece. Fold foil securely and cook on the grill for 20-30 minutes. Can also be cooked in a 350°F (180°C) oven for 15-20 minutes or until fish flakes when fork-tested.

Braised Salmon Steaks

Ingredients:

4 **salmon** steaks
   (6-8 oz/170-225 g ea)
3 Tbsp (45 ml) vegetable
   oil
1 large or 2 small **fennel
   bulbs** (about 1 lb/454 g),
   trim base and stocks,
   thinly slice
3 **garlic clove**s, minced
2 tsp (10 ml) dried **thyme**
   OR 2 Tbsp (30 ml)
   chopped fresh
½ tsp (2 ml) **celery seeds**
½ tsp (2 ml) **salt**
¼ tsp (1 ml) freshly
   ground black **pepper**
Thyme OR **parsley** sprigs

Method:

Preheat oven to 375°F
(190°C). Rinse salmon and pat
dry. In a large skillet, over
medium heat add oil and sauté
fennel and garlic, stirring
occasionally until vegetables
begin to soften, about
5 minutes, remove and set
aside. In a small bowl combine
thyme, celery seeds, salt and
pepper. Rub on both sides of
salmon. Braise steaks in hot
skillet just until nicely
browned, about 1 minute each
side. Remove from skillet.
Lightly oil a baking dish. Place
fennel and garlic mixture on
bottom and salmon steaks on
top in a single layer. Place a
sprig of thyme on each steak, if
desired. Cover dish with foil
and bake until fish flakes when
fork-tested, approximately
10-15 minutes. Place steaks and
fennel mixture on a warmed
serving platter and garnish
with additional thyme sprigs or
parsley. Serve with grilled
roasted potatoes. Serves 4.

Westcoast Soused Salmon

Ingredients:
Salmon
Rind of one **lemon**, thinly
   pared
½ tsp (2 ml) whole **allspice**
1 tsp (5 ml) whole **cloves**
½ tsp (2 ml) dried **thyme**
2 tsp (10 ml) **parsley**,
   chopped
3 bay leaves
1 tsp (5 ml) **pepper corns**,
   grated
1 tsp (5 ml) **salt**
1 cup (250 ml) **vinegar**
1 cup (250 ml) **water**

Method:
Prepare salmon by washing in slightly salted water. Cut salmon into serving size pieces and place in a baking dish. Tie next seven ingredients in a double thickness of cheesecloth or muslin and place in baking dish with salmon. Combine salt with vinegar and water, pour over fish and spices. Cover baking dish, cook in a 200°F (100°C) oven for 1 ½ hours or until fish flakes when fork-tested. Fish may be served hot or served cold by leaving in cooking liquid in refrigerator.

Linda's Baked Salmon

Ingredients:
Salmon
¼ cup (60 ml) **butter** OR
   margarine, melted
1 **clove garlic**, minced
1 small **onion**, chopped fine
2 Tbsp (30 ml) **lemon juice**
2 tsp (10 ml) **dill**
1 tsp (5 ml) **salt** or to taste
½ tsp (2 ml) **pepper** or to
   taste

Method:
Preheat oven to 425°F (220°C). Rinse salmon, pat dry. In a small bowl, mix all ingredients and spread over salmon. Roll tightly in foil. Bake at 425°F (220°C), approximately 10 minutes per inch (2.5 cm) at thickest part, add 5 minutes to total cooking time for heat to penetrate foil. Salmon should be moist and flake when fork tested. Serve with Raspberry Salsa on page 13.

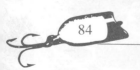

Salmon Stuffed with Shrimp & Rice

Ingredients:

4-5 lbs (2-2.5 kg) **salmon**
¼ cup (60 ml) **butter**
1 small **onion**, chopped
   fine
½ cup (125 ml) **celery**,
   finely chopped
½ cup (125 ml)
   mushrooms, sliced
1 cup (250 ml) cooked **rice**
1 can (4 ½ oz / 128 ml)
   shrimp, drained and
   chopped
¼ cup (60 ml) **parsley**,
   chopped
¼ tsp (1 ml) dried leaf
   thyme, crumbled
Salt and **pepper** to taste
2 **egg** yolks, beaten
2 Tbsp (30 ml) **butter**,
   melted

Method:

Rinse fish under cold running water and pat dry. Make stuffing by melting butter in a skillet. Add onion and celery and cook until onion is yellow. Add mushrooms and cook for 1 minute, set aside. In a bowl combine rice, shrimp, parsley, thyme, salt and pepper. Add to onion and celery mixture and toss lightly to mix. Add beaten egg yolks and toss lightly again to mix. Lightly stuff fish. Sew opening closed with heavy thread. Lightly grease a large piece of foil to fit on baking sheet. Lay fish on foil and baste with melted butter. Bake at 425°F (220°C), approximately 10 minutes per inch (2.5 cm) at thickest part. Salmon should be moist and flake when fork tested.

Joy's Baked Salmon

Contributed by Joy Cowper-Smith, Victoria, B.C., Canada

Ingredients:
- **Salmon**: fillets, steaks, OR whole
- **Mayonnaise**
- **Brown sugar**
- **Salt** to taste
- Dry Onion **Soup mix**

Method:

Line a baking dish with foil. Lay fish on foil (if using whole fish, lay out flat). Spread mayonnaise over fish then sprinkle with brown sugar, salt and soup mix. Bake, uncovered at 425°F (220°C), about 10 minutes per inch (2.5 cm) at thickest part. Salmon should be moist and flake when fork tested.

Donna's Salmon á lá King

Ingredients:
- 2 Tbsp (30 ml) **margarine**
- 1 Tbsp (15 ml) **onion**, chopped
- 1 Tbsp (15 ml) green **pepper**, chopped
- 1 Tbsp (15 ml) **pimento**, chopped
- 3 Tbsp (45 ml) all-purpose **flour**
- 2 cups (500 ml) **milk**
- **Salt**, **pepper**, **paprika** to taste
- 1 can (8 oz/225 g) **salmon**, drained and flaked
- ½-1 cup (125-250 ml) button **mushrooms**

Method:

Melt margarine over hot water in double boiler. Add onions, green pepper and pimento. Cook until tender. Blend in flour until a smooth paste is formed and flour absorbed. Cook for 2-3 minutes. Slowly stir in milk, salt, pepper, and paprika. Cook, stirring constantly, until thick and smooth. Add salmon and mushrooms. Heat and serve in patty (pastry) shells, over toast or steamed rice. Serves 4.

Laredo Sound Salmon Omelet

Ingredients:
- 4 **eggs**, slightly beaten
- ¼ cup (60 ml) **milk**
- 2 Tbsp (30 ml) **butter** OR **margarine**
- ¼ tsp (1 ml) **salt**
- 2 Tbsp (30 ml) green **onion**, minced
- 2 Tbsp (30 ml) **parsley**, minced
- 8 oz (225 g) cooked **salmon**, flaked

Method:
Lightly mix eggs, milk in a bowl. Melt butter in skillet over medium heat. Pour in egg mixture and cook until edges set, but still creamy, gently lifting edges and tilting pan so uncooked egg can run to the bottom. Mix together salt, green onion, parsley, and salmon and add to egg mixture. Cook until eggs set. Serves 2.

Supreme Salmon Hash

Ingredients:
- 1 small green **pepper**, chopped
- 4 oz (115 g) **mushrooms**, chopped
- ¼ cup (60 ml) **onion**, minced
- 2 Tbsp (30 ml) **butter** OR **margarine**
- 1 can (1 lb / 454 g) **salmon**, flaked, reserve liquid
- 1 tsp (5 ml) steak **sauce**
- ¼ tsp (1 ml) **salt**
- ⅛ tsp (.5 ml) **pepper**
- **Paprika**
- ½ cup (125 ml) **sour cream**
- 2 cups (500 ml) seasoned mashed **potatoes**

Method:
Sauté green pepper, mushrooms and onion 3-4 minutes in butter over medium high heat in cast iron fry pan. Add liquid from salmon into sautéed mixture. Add flaked salmon, steak sauce, salt, pepper and ¼ tsp (1 ml) paprika to mixture. Stir well. Place mixture in shallow broiler-proof dish. Spread sour cream on top of salmon mixture and mashed potatoes around edge. Sprinkle top with paprika and broil 4 inch (10 cm) from heat for 5-6 minutes or until lightly browned. Serves 4.

Salmon Filled Biscuits

Ingredients:
1 can (7 ½ oz / 215 g) **salmon**
2 hard-boiled **eggs**, chopped
⅓ cup (80 ml) **mayonnaise**
2 green **onions**, chopped
3 Tbsp (45 ml) **parsley**, chopped
1 tsp (5 ml) **lemon juice**
½ tsp (2 ml) **dill**, chopped
Pepper
1 pkg refrigerated biscuit dough OR croissant roll dough

Method:
In a medium-size bowl, mash salmon with juices and bones. Combine the rest of the ingredients (except dough) into the salmon. Separate the dough into two squares, gently pressing the perforations to seal. Cut each square into quarters. Place 3 Tbsp (45 ml) of the mixture into the center of each square and fold into a triangle. Pinch to seal edges. Place on an ungreased baking sheet and bake at 375°F (190°C) for 15-20 minutes or until golden brown and puffy.

Grammy's Instant Fish Cakes

Contributed by Mae Hood, Ashcroft, B.C., Canada

Ingredients:
1 can (7 ½ oz / 213 g) **salmon**, drained
1 cup (250 ml) prepared instant mashed **potatoes**
¼ cup (60 ml) **onion**, finely chopped
¼ cup (60 ml) **parsley**, chopped
Salt and **pepper** to taste
Bread crumbs, dried, crushed fine
Oil

Method:
Combine all ingredients other than the breadcrumbs and oil, mixing very thoroughly. Fill a ¼ cup (60 ml) measuring cup with mixture. Form into ½ inch (1 cm) thick patties, coat lightly with breadcrumbs. Fry on preheated cast iron fry pan which has been lightly coated with oil. Fry until golden on both sides, approximately 3 minutes per side. Makes 5 fish cakes.

Creamed Salmon on Toast

Contributed by Sharon Johnson, Esperanza, B.C., Canada

Ingredients:
- 2 cups (500 ml) **White Sauce**, see recipe on page 90
- 2 cups (500 ml) cooked, left-over **fish**
- **Salt** and **pepper** to taste
- ½ cup (125 ml) **frozen peas**
- **Toast**

Method:
Prepare white sauce in heavy fry pan. Add broken chunks of fish, salt, pepper and peas. Gently heat to boiling. Serve over toast.

Oregon Salmon Loaf

Ingredients:
- 1 can (1 lb / 454 g) **salmon** or fresh cooked
- 1 can (10 oz / 284 ml) cream of mushroom **soup**
- 1 cup (250 ml) dry **bread crumbs**, crushed fine
- 2 **eggs**, slightly beaten
- ½ cup (125 ml) **onion**, chopped
- 1 Tbsp (15 ml) **lemon juice**
- **Milk** (optional)

Method:
In a large mixing bowl, combine all ingredients with juice from the canned salmon or a little milk to moisten. Place mixture in a well-greased loaf pan. Bake in a 375°F (190°C) oven for about 1 hour. Place on a warm serving platter and garnish as desired. Serve with rice and Mushroom Sauce, see recipe on page 10.

Salmon Loaf Supreme

Ingredients:
- 1 can (1 lb / 454 g) **salmon**
- 2 Tbsp (30 ml) **lemon juice**
- 2 **eggs**, slightly beaten
- 1 cup (250 ml) soft **bread crumbs**
- 2 Tbsp (30 ml) **onion**, chopped
- ½ tsp (2 ml) **salt**
- 2 cups (500 ml) **biscuit mix**
- 10 pimento stuffed green **olives**

Method:

Place salmon, with juice, in a bowl; remove bones and skin. Break salmon into flakes with a fork. Add lemon juice, eggs, bread crumbs, onion and salt; mix thoroughly. Make dough with biscuit mix according to package directions, roll out on waxed paper into a 9" x 12" (23 x 30 cm) oblong. Press olives into dough along one of the 9" (23 cm) ends only. Spread salmon mixture over the dough. Starting at the 9" (23 cm) end with the olives, roll as for cinnamon rolls, pinching edges together to seal. Place roll on a double thickness of waxed paper, 5" x 12" (13 x 30 cm), with seam side down. Lift into greased 9" x 5" x 3" (23 x 13 x 7.5 cm) loaf pan. Place in a 400°F (200°C) oven and bake for 40-50 minutes. When done place on warmed serving platter. Serve with white sauce and peas.

White Sauce

Ingredients:
- 4 Tbsp (60 ml) **butter**
- 4 Tbsp (60 ml) **flour**
- 2 ½ cups (625 ml) **milk**
- 1 can (14 oz / 398 ml) **peas**, drained
- **Salt** and **pepper** to taste

Method:

In heavy fry pan over medium heat, melt butter, stir in flour until absorbed. Cook 2-3 minutes, stirring occasionally. Remove pan from heat. Slowly stir in milk. Return pan to heat, stirring constantly until sauce is smooth, boiling and thickened. Heat peas in the sauce, season with salt and pepper. Serve with salmon loaf.

Dilled Salmon Loaf

Ingredients:
- 2 cans (8 oz / 225 g) **salmon**
- 1 lb (454 g) creamed **cottage cheese**
- ½ cup (125 ml) soft **bread crumbs**
- ¼ cup (60 ml) **bran**
- ¼ cup (60 ml) **wheat germ**
- ¼ cup (60 ml) green **onion**, finely chopped
- 1 Tbsp (15 ml) **lemon juice**
- 1 **egg**, beaten
- ½ tsp (2 ml) **salt**
- Dash **pepper** and **nutmeg**
- 6 small garlic dill **pickles**

Method:

In a medium-size mixing bowl mash salmon, including bones, skin and juices. Add remaining ingredients, except pickles, and mix well. Line a 9" x 4" x 3" (23 x 10 x 7.5 cm) pan with foil. Spread half of the mixture in the pan. Arrange dill pickles on top, then spread remaining mixture on top of pickles. Bake in a 325°F (160°C) oven for 1 hour. Serve sliced.

Matsqui Fish Loaf

Contributed by Mrs. Lumley, Abbotsford, B.C., Canada

Ingredients:
- 2 **eggs**, beaten
- 1 cup (250 ml) **milk**
- ¼ cup **onion**, chopped
- ¼ tsp **celery salt**
- Dash **pepper**, **paprika**
- ½ tsp (2 ml) **salt** or to taste
- 1 Tbsp (15 ml) **lemon juice**
- 2 cups (500 ml) soft **bread crumbs**
- 2 ½ cups (625 ml) canned **salmon** OR fresh cooked

Method:

In a medium size bowl, beat eggs and milk together. Stir in onion and seasonings. Add bread crumbs and fish with juice. Mix well. Place fish mixture into lightly-greased loaf pan. Sprinkle with paprika. Set loaf pan in a larger pan of hot water. Bake in a 350°F (180°C) oven for about 40 minutes. Don't overbake.

Molded Salmon Loaf

IIngredients:
- 2 cups (500 ml) canned **salmon**, skin removed, flaked
- 2 cups (500 ml) fine, soft **bread crumbs**
- 2 **eggs**, beaten
- 1 cup (250 ml) **White Sauce**, see recipe on page 90
- 1 Tbsp (15 ml) **onion**, finely minced
- 1 tsp (5 ml) **lemon juice**

Method:
Place salmon in a bowl, crush bones. Combine with remaining ingredients mixing well, chill. Lightly coat baking sheet with cooking spray. Turn fish mixture onto baking sheet and mold into fish shape. Bake in a 350°F (180°C) oven for 30 minutes or until firm. Remove to a serving platter. Using a pastry tube pipe mayonnaise onto fish to represent scales, sliced stuffed olive for the eye. Garnish with lemon slices and parsley. Chill. Serves 6.

Cape Meares Scalloped Salmon

Ingredients:
- 1 can (1 lb/454 g) **salmon**
- **Milk**
- 1 Tbsp (15 ml) instant minced **onion**
- Few sprigs of **parsley**, chopped
- ¼ tsp (1 ml) ground **thyme**
- 1 tsp (5 ml) **salt**
- ⅛ tsp (.5 ml) **pepper**
- 1 ½ cup (375 ml) soda **cracker crumbs**, coarse crushed
- 3 Tbsp (45 ml) **butter** OR **margarine**

Method:
Drain liquid from salmon into a measuring cup and add milk to make 1 cup (250 ml). In a bowl, flake salmon, add liquid and seasonings; mix lightly. Butter a 9" (23 cm) pie pan, sprinkle a layer of cracker crumbs on bottom and sides. Save some crumbs for top. Spoon mixture on crumbs, dot with 1 Tbsp (15 ml) of butter. Sprinkle remaining crumbs and dot with remaining butter. Bake in a 400°F (200°C) oven for about 15 minutes until nicely browned and hot.

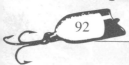

Smoked Salmon Roulade

Ingredients:

- 1 ¼ cups (310 ml) **milk**
- 1 **onion**, chopped
- 2 Tbsp (30 ml) **butter** OR **margarine**
- 2 Tbsp (30 ml) **flour**
- ½ tsp (2 ml) **dill weed**
- ½ tsp (2 ml) **salt**
- ½ tsp (2 ml) **lemon pepper**
- 10 **eggs**, separated
- ½ cup (125 ml) Edam **cheese**, grated
- 1 ½ cups (375 ml) smoked **salmon**, flaked
- 2 Tbsp (30 ml) green **onion**, minced

Method:

Preheat oven to 400°F (200°C). In a small pot, combine milk and onion and heat. In a medium saucepan melt butter, stir in flour to make a roux (paste) and remove from heat. Strain milk, discard onion. Gradually stir milk into roux and heat until smooth and thickened. Add seasonings and slightly beaten egg yolks, stirring continually while cooking for one minute. Stir in cheese, salmon and green onion until cheese melts. Remove from heat. Beat egg whites until stiff, but not dry; fold gently into sauce. Line a 15" x 10" (40 x 25 cm) cookie sheet with waxed paper. Gently spread mixture evenly in pan. Bake for about 15-18 minutes or until browned and set. Lay a clean tea towel over the top and invert onto a counter, gently peel back wax paper, roll up from short end to make a tight even roll.

Sauce

Ingredients:

- 2 Tbsp (30 ml) **butter** OR **margarine**
- 2 Tbsp (30 ml) **flour**
- ¾ cup (175 ml) **chicken stock**
- ½ cup (125 ml) **milk**
- ½ tsp (2 ml) **lemon pepper**
- 3 Tbsp (45 ml) **capers**, drained

Method:

Melt margarine over medium heat in a small saucepan. Stir in flour to make a roux (paste). Gradually stir in stock and milk. Heat and stir until sauce is smooth and thickened. Stir in lemon pepper and capers. Ladle sauce onto warm serving plates and place a slice of roll on top. Serves 6.

Creamy Pasta & Salmon Salad

Contributed by Tammy Wall, Harrison Hot Springs, B.C., Canada

Ingredients:
- 2 cups (500 ml) cooked shell **pasta**
- 1 can (7 oz / 199 ml) **salmon**, drained
- ½ cup (125 ml) Snow or Sugar **peas**, cut bite-size
- ½ cup (125 ml) red **pepper**, julienned
- ¼ cup (60 ml) **pecans**, chopped

Dressing

Ingredients:
- ½ cup (125 ml) **sour cream**
- ½ cup (125 ml) **mayonnaise**
- 2 tsp (10 ml) **lemon juice**
- ⅛ tsp (.5 ml) **garlic powder**
- ⅛ tsp (.5 ml) **pepper**
- Dash **Tabasco sauce**

Method:
In a small bowl combine dressing ingredients. In a separate bowl add pasta and remaining ingredients, pour dressing over pasta and toss.

Beans and Salmon Salad

Ingredients:
- 1 can (19 oz / 540 ml) white navy **beans** OR black **beans**, drained, rinsed
- ½ cup (125 ml) **parsley**, chopped
- 4 green **onions**, thinly sliced
- 2 stalks **celery**, sliced
- ⅓ cup (80 ml) sweet red **pepper**, diced
- 2 **cloves garlic**, minced
- ⅓ cup (80 ml) **lemon juice**
- ⅓ cup (80 ml) **olive oil**
- ½ tsp (2 ml) dry **mustard**
- **Salt** and **pepper** to taste
- 1 can (8 oz / 225 g) **salmon**
- Leaf **lettuce**

Method:
In a glass bowl toss together beans, parsley, onion, celery and red pepper. In a small bowl, mix together garlic, lemon juice, oil, mustard, salt and pepper. Pour over bean mixture, stir and cover. Refrigerate over night or at least 8 hours. Remove beans from refrigerator and bring to room temperature. Drain salmon, removing skin. Break salmon into chunks, mashing bones if necessary. Toss bean mixture and salmon together. Serve on lettuce lined plates. Serves 4.

Salmon Cucumber Salad

Ingredients:
- 2 **cucumbers**, peeled
- 1 ¼ tsp (6 ml) **salt**, divided
- ¼ tsp (1 ml) **pepper**
- 1 can or leftover cooked **salmon** to equal 1 lb (454 g), flaked
- ¾ cup (175 ml) **sour cream**
- 1 Tbsp (15 ml) **lemon juice**
- 2 Tbsp (30 ml) **chives** OR green **onion**, minced

Method:
Cut cucumber into quarters lengthwise. Remove seeds, cut into thin slices. Sprinkle with 1 tsp (5 ml) salt and the pepper. Let stand for 30 minutes. Drain well and mix lightly with the salmon. (If using canned salmon, drain.) Mix sour cream, lemon juice and remaining salt. Pour over cucumber mixture and sprinkle with chives. Serves 4.

Marinated Salmon Salad

Ingredients:
- 1 can or leftover cooked **salmon** to equal 1 lb (454 g)
- 1 cup (250 ml) **sour cream**
- ½ tsp (2 ml) **salt**
- 2 Tbsp (30 ml) **lemon juice**
- ¼ cup (60 ml) red **onion**, minced
- **Lettuce**
- ¼ cup (60 ml) green **onion**, minced
- 2 Tbsp (30 ml) **parsley**, chopped
- 5 whole **allspice**, cracked fine

Method:
Place chunked salmon in deep glass dish. In a separate bowl, mix sour cream, salt, lemon juice, and minced red onion together and pour over salmon. Stir, cover and chill at least one hour. Serve on lettuce leaf. Garnish with red onion slices and a mixture of green onion and parsley. Sprinkle lightly with allspice. Serves 4.

Whidbey Island Salmon and Pasta Salad

Ingredients:

8 oz (225 g) dry **pasta** spirals or shells

1 lb (454 g) **salmon** fillets or steaks

Salt and **pepper** to taste

3 Tbsp (45 ml) **tarragon** leaves, minced

2 Tbsp (30 ml) green **onion**, minced

1 Tbsp (15 ml) **lemon juice**

¼ cup (60 ml) plain, non-fat **yogurt**

8 oz (225 g) cherry **tomatoes**

Lettuce

Method:

Preheat oven to 400°F (200°C). Cook pasta per package directions. Drain pasta, then rinse with cold water, drain again. Set aside. Rinse fillets and pat dry. Season both sides of fillet with salt and pepper. Place on a lightly oiled baking sheet and bake until just opaque, about 8-12 minutes or until opaque and fish flakes when fork-tested. Set aside. When fillet or steak is cooled, skin and debone, if needed. Break fish into large chunks. Mix tarragon, green onion, lemon juice, yogurt, salt and pepper in a large bowl. Add well-drained pasta, toss to coat evenly. Add salmon and halved, stemmed tomatoes. Stir gently so as not to break up salmon. Cover and refrigerate. Serve on a lettuce leaf for color.

SEAFOOD

Salmon Party Ball 99

Microwaved Citrus Salmon 81

Delicious Smoked Salmon
Cheesecake Dip 106

Altoona Salmon and Corn Pie 113

Matsqui Fish Loaf 91

Salmon and Rice Casserole

Ingredients:
- 1 can or leftover cooked
  salmon to equal 1 lb
  (454 g)
- 2 cups (500 ml) cooked
  rice
- 1 cup (250 ml) **celery**,
  thinly sliced
- ½ cup (125 ml) **parsley**,
  chopped
- ¼ cup (60 ml) **olive**s,
  sliced
- ½ cup (125 ml)
  mayonnaise
- ¼ cup (60 ml) **sour cream**
- 2 Tbsp (30 ml) **lemon juice**
- **Salt** and **pepper**
- ⅓ cup (80 ml) **almonds**,
  thinly sliced
- **Parmesan cheese**, grated
- **Paprika**

Method:

In a medium bowl, break salmon into chunks. Stir in rice, celery, parsley and olives. In a small bowl mix mayonnaise, sour cream and lemon juice. Add salt and pepper to taste. Pour over salmon mixture and toss lightly. Divide into 6 well-greased shallow 1 cup (250 ml) casserole or baking dishes. Sprinkle with a mixture of almonds, cheese and paprika. Bake in 400°F (200°C) oven for 15-20 minutes, or until heated and golden brown. Serves 6.

There are many proven health benefits of including fish in your diet. Eating fish can reduce your chances of suffering a stroke. The Heart Association recommends eating two servings of fish a week.

Salmon Crepes Delmonico

Contributed by Marjie Spani, North Vancouver, B.C., Canada

Crepe Ingredients:
- ½ cup (125 ml) **flour**
- ¼ tsp (1 ml) **salt**
- ½ cup (125 ml) **milk**
- 2 **egg whites**, beaten slightly
- **Oil** for frying

Filling Ingredients:
- 1 can (7 ¾ oz / 220 g) **salmon**, drained and flaked
- 1 cup (250 ml) cream-style **cottage cheese**
- ¼ tsp (1 ml) **salt**
- 2 **egg yolks**
- 1 Tbsp (15 ml) fresh **chives**, chopped OR ½ tsp (2 ml) dried **dill weed**
- 1 cup (250 ml) **sour cream**
- **Parsley**

Crepes

Method:
Combine flour and salt in a bowl. In a separate bowl combine milk and egg whites; stir into flour mixture until smooth. Let batter rest for 30 minutes. Stir batter. Thin with milk if necessary. The consistency of the batter should be thinner than a pancake batter. Heat a 6 inch (15 cm) crepe pan. Put ½ tsp (2 ml) oil in pan and heat until it sizzles. Pour about 2 Tbsp (30 ml) of batter into pan and tip until evenly coated. Cook over moderate heat until crepe is browned on one side, about 1 minute. Turn over and brown other side. Shake cooked crepe onto a towel and cover with wax paper until ready to serve. Grease pan slightly between crepes.

Filling

Method:
Combine salmon, cottage cheese, salt, egg yolks and chives, or dill weed, in a mixing bowl. Spread ¼ cup (60 ml) of mixture on each crepe, making sure attractive side of crepe is on outside and roll up. Arrange side by side in a buttered baking dish, heat in a 350°F (180°C) oven for 12-15 minutes. Arrange on heated serving platter with seam side down. Spoon a ribbon of sour cream on top and garnish with parsley. Serves 4.

Pacific Rim Salmon Wraps

Ingredients:
- ⅓ cup (80 ml) **dill cream cheese**, room temperature
- 4 flour **tortillas**
- 7 oz (200 g) smoked **salmon**, crumbled
- 2 Tbsp (30 l) **seafood sauce**
- 1 cups (250 ml) Swiss **cheese**, grated
- 4 green **onions**, sliced
- 2 **tomatoes**, chopped and cored
- **Lettuce**, shredded
- **Salt** and **pepper** to taste

Method:

Spread cream cheese in a 2 inch (5 cm) wide band through centre of tortilla. Mix together salmon and seafood sauce, spread on top of cream cheese. Add Swiss cheese, onions, tomatoes and top with lettuce. Fold bottom end up and fold over both sides. Serve.

Salmon Party Ball

Contributed by Barb Hood, Ashcroft, B.C., Canada

Ingredients:
- 8 oz (225 g) **cream cheese**, room temperature
- 1 cup (250 ml) cooked or canned **salmon**, drained
- 1 Tbsp (15 ml) **lemon juice**
- 2 tsp (10 ml) **onion**, grated
- 1 tsp (5 ml) prepared **horseradish**
- ¼ tsp (1 ml) **salt**
- ¼ tsp (1 ml) **liquid smoke** (optional)
- ½ cup (125 ml) **nuts**, chopped
- 3 Tbsp (45 ml) **parsley**, snipped

Method:

In a bowl, combine first 7 ingredients. Cover, chill about 1 hour. Shape into ball. Roll ball in mixture of chopped nuts and snipped parsley. Chill for several hours. Serve with crackers.

Salmon Frittata

Ingredients:

1 can (6 ½ oz / 175 g) **salmon**, boned and skinned

2 Tbsp (30 ml) **butter** OR **margarine**

1 cup (250 ml) **mushrooms**, sliced

½ cup (125 ml) **celery**, sliced

¼ cup (60 ml) green **onion**s, chopped

¼ cup (60 ml) green **pepper**, slivered

2 **clove**s **garlic**, minced

¼ tsp (1 ml) **basil**

¼ tsp (1 ml) **oregano**

Salt and **pepper** to taste

8 **eggs**

¼ cup (60 ml) **milk**

Method:

In a small bowl, drain salmon and separate with a fork into chunks. Melt butter in a large non-stick fry pan. Sauté mushrooms, celery, green onion, green pepper, garlic, herbs, salt and pepper over high heat until vegetables are tender-crisp. Remove from heat. In a medium bowl, beat together eggs and milk then pour over vegetables in pan. Place salmon on top of eggs. Cover the pan and cook over medium-low heat for 10-15 minutes or until eggs are set. You can gently lift edge of cooked egg and tip pan so uncooked egg flows underneath. Cut into wedges. Serves 6.

Smoked Salmon Quiche

Ingredients:

Pastry

3 large **eggs**

1 cup (250 ml) **milk**

2 tsp (10 ml) Dijon **mustard**

2 Tbsp (30 ml) fresh **dill**, chopped OR ¼ tsp (1 ml) dried **dill weed**

¼ tsp (1 ml) **salt**

¼ tsp (1 ml) **pepper**

¼ cup (60 ml) **onion**, diced

4 oz (100 g) smoked **salmon**, crumbled

1 cup (250 ml) Swiss **cheese**, shredded

1 cup (250 ml) **asparagus** OR **broccoli**, chopped

Method:

Loosely line a 9 inch (23 cm) quiche or pie pan with pastry leaving a 1 ½ inch (4 cm) overhang to turn inside rim and flute edges. Prick crust in several places, pat out air bubbles. Bake at 450°F (230°C) for 10-12 minutes or until golden brown. Remove, cool. Meanwhile prepare quiche by whisking together the eggs. Stir in milk, mustard, seasonings, onion, salmon, ½ cup (125 ml) cheese and asparagus (or broccoli). Pour into prepared pastry and sprinkle with remaining cheese. Bake at 375°F (190°C) for 30-35 minutes or until knife inserted in center comes out clean. Cool on rack for 10 minutes before serving.

Did you know that barbecues are Biblical? "When (the disciples) stepped ashore, they saw a charcoal fire there with fish on it and some bread. Then Jesus said to them, Bring some of the fish you have just caught." John 21:9,10

Checleset Bay Salmon Balls in Vegetable Sauce

Ingredients:

2 Tbsp (30 ml) **butter** OR **margarine**

½ cup (125 ml) **onion**, chopped

½ cup (125 ml) **celery**, chopped

1 can (10 oz/284 ml) vegetable **soup**

¾ cup (175 ml) **water**

1 can (8 oz/225 g) **salmon**, drained, reserved OR 1 cup (250 ml) cooked, leftover **salmon**

½ cup (125 ml) soft **bread crumbs**

2 **eggs**, well beaten

¼ tsp (1 ml) **lemon rind**, grated

½ tsp (2 ml) dry **mustard**

½ tsp (2 ml) **Worcestershire sauce**

¼ tsp (1 ml) **salt**

¾ cup (175 ml) **bread crumbs**, dried, crushed fine

Method:

In a large heavy pot, melt butter and sauté onion and celery until just tender. Add soup, water and reserved juice from salmon. Keep hot. In medium size bowl mix salmon with next 6 ingredients and form into 8 balls. Roll each in dried bread crumbs. Drop into hot soup mixture and cover. Simmer 12 minutes. Serve in the center of a hot rice ring or with fluffy mashed potatoes. Serves 4.

North Bay Salmon Lasagne

Ingredients:
- ¼ cup (60 ml) **olive oil**
- 1 medium **onion**, chopped fine
- 1 **garlic clove**, minced
- 2 cans (16 oz / 455 ml ea) **tomatoes**, chopped
- 1 can (6 oz / 170 ml) **tomato paste**
- **Salt** and **pepper** to taste
- 1 tsp (5 ml) **basil**
- ½ tsp (2 ml) **oregano**
- ¼ cup (60 ml) **parsley**, chopped
- 1 can (1 lb / 454 g) **salmon**, drained, reserve juice, flaked
- 1 lb (454 g) broad spinach **noodles** OR regular lasagne **noodles**
- 8 oz (225 g) mozzarella **cheese**, sliced
- 1 lb (454 g) **ricotta** OR creamed **cottage cheese**
- ½ cup (125 ml) **Parmesan cheese**, grated

Method:

Heat oil in a large saucepan, cook onion and garlic until soft. Add tomatoes, paste, salt, pepper, basil, oregano, parsley and reserved juice from salmon, cover. Let simmer for 30 minutes. Stir frequently. Cook and thoroughly drain noodles according to package directions. In a buttered, shallow 2 qt (2 l) baking dish, spread ¼ of the sauce on bottom. Top with a layer of noodles, then mozzarella cheese, ricotta or cottage cheese, and a layer of salmon; sprinkle with Parmesan cheese. Repeat layering, ending with noodles. Top with remaining sauce and sprinkle with Parmesan cheese. Bake uncovered in a 350°F (180°C) oven about 30 minutes, until well browned and bubbly. Serves 6-8.

Curried Salmon

Ingredients:
- ¼ cup (60 ml) **butter** OR **margarine**
- 1 small **onion**, minced
- 1 tsp (5 ml) **curry powder**
- 2 tsp (10 ml) **paprika**
- ¼ tsp (1 ml) **ginger**
- **Salt** to taste
- 1 tsp (5 ml) **cumin seed**
- ¼ cup (60 ml) **flour**
- 1 ½ cups (375 ml) **milk**
- 1 can (1 lb / 454 g) canned **salmon**, reserve juice
- ½ cup (125 ml) heavy **cream**
- Hot cooked **rice**

Method:

In heavy fry pan, over medium heat, melt butter, add onion and sauté for 2-3 minutes. Add curry powder, paprika, ginger, salt, cumin seed and sauté 1 minute longer. Blend the flour into the onion mixture and cook for 3 minutes until all the flour is absorbed. Add milk gradually, stirring constantly until thickened and smooth. Stir in the liquid from the canned salmon. Flake the salmon and add to mixture. Cover and cook for 10 minutes. Stir in cream. Continue stirring until hot, but not boiling. On a warmed serving platter, pour curried salmon over rice or serve separately. Serves 4.

Two fishermen travel 100 miles to try out a new fishing spot. They buy a variety of bait and lures and rent a boat. After a long day of fishing, the two fishermen return to the dock. The first fisherman pulls their only catch from the live well, a scrawny bass just legal size. He says, "Boy! This fish cost us about $75." The second fisherman says, "Well, it's a good thing we didn't catch any more."

Klipsan Beach Salmon Muffins

Ingredients:
- 2 cups (500 ml) **salmon**, canned or fresh cooked, mashed
- 1 cup (250 ml) fresh **bread crumbs**
- ½ tsp (2 ml) **salt** or to taste
- ⅛ tsp (.5 ml) **pepper**
- 1 tsp (5 ml) **Accent** (optional)
- 2 **eggs**, beaten
- ¾ cup (175 ml) **milk**
- 1 tsp (5 ml) **lemon juice**
- 1 Tbsp (15 ml) **onion**, minced

Method:
Place all ingredients in a large bowl and mix well. Spray muffin pans with non-stick cooking spray. Place ½ to ¾ cup (125-175 ml) mixture in muffin cups. Bake in a 350°F (180°C) oven for 25 minutes until toothpick inserted in center comes out clean.

Seattle Salmon Soufflé

Ingredients:
- 1 can (8 oz/225 g) **salmon**, drain, reserve liquid
- 1 cup (250 ml) reserved **salmon** juice + **milk**
- 4 soda **crackers**
- 2 **eggs**, separated
- 1 Tbsp (15 ml) **butter**, melted
- **Salt** and **pepper** to taste
- **Cracker crumbs**, finely crushed

Method:
In a bowl, combine salmon juice and milk. Add crackers, soak for ½ hour. In a separate bowl flake salmon. Add well beaten egg yolks, melted butter, salt and pepper to salmon. Mix until well blended. Add soaked crackers to fish mixture, blend well. Gently fold in stiffly beaten egg whites. Grease a 1 qt (1 l) casserole dish, dust with crumbs. Pour fish mixture into casserole, bake 1 hour in a 325°F (160°C) oven until puffy and golden.

Delicious Smoked Salmon Cheesecake Spread

Contributed by Elfriede Dyck, Abbotsford, B.C., Canada

Base

Ingredients:
- ½ cup (125 ml) dried **bread crumbs**, crushed fine
- 1 Tbsp (15 ml) **butter**, melted
- 1 tsp (5 ml) dried **dill**

Method:

Combine bread crumbs, melted butter and dill in a bowl. Press mixture in a spring-form pan, and bake in a 350°F (180°C) oven for 5-7 minutes or until golden brown. Set aside.

Filling

Ingredients:
- 1 Tbsp (15 ml) **butter**
- 1 small **onion**, chopped fine
- 3 pkgs **cream cheese** (8 oz / 225 g ea) at room temperature
- 3 large **eggs**
- ⅓ cup (80 ml) light **cream**
- **Salt** to taste
- 8 oz (225 g) smoked **salmon**
- 1 cup (250 ml) Swiss **cheese**, grated

Method:

Melt butter in a small fry pan and sauté onion until just turning brown. Set aside to cool. Beat cream cheese, eggs, cream and salt in a bowl until creamy. Chop salmon into coarse chunks, and place into small bowl, mix in onion and Swiss cheese; turn into cream mixture. Pour over the cooked base in the spring-form pan. Bake in a 300°F (150°C) oven for 75 minutes. Turn heat off and slightly open oven door. Let cheesecake cool in oven for 1 hour. Remove from oven and place in refrigerator for at least 2 hours before removing from spring-form pan. Serve at room temperature with crackers. Delicious! Freezes well.

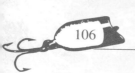

Salmon Newburg

Ingredients:
- ½ cup (125 ml) **butter**
- 6 Tbsp (90 ml) all-purpose **flour**
- 4 cups (1 l) **cream**
- 5 Tbsp (75 ml) **Parmesan cheese**, grated
- 3 Tbsp (45 ml) **paprika**
- 1 tsp (5 ml) dry **mustard**
- **Salt** and **cayenne** to taste
- 6 **egg yolks**, well beaten
- 4 Tbsp (60 ml) **brandy**
- 4 Tbsp (60 ml) dry **Sherry**
- 6 cups (1.5 l) cooked **salmon**, flaked

Method:

In a saucepan, melt butter and stir in flour to make a roux (paste). Stir constantly for 1-2 minutes. Do not brown the roux. Heat the cream and gradually add to the roux, stirring constantly. Cook until sauce is thick and smooth. Add Parmesan cheese, paprika, dry mustard, salt and cayenne. Place the egg yolks in the top of a double boiler and pour the sauce slowly over the egg yolks. Cook over a double boiler, stirring, for 3 minutes. Stir in brandy, Sherry and salmon. Heat, but do not boil. To serve, keep warm by setting serving dish in hot water on a warming tray.

Stranger than fiction:

What fish has her own fishing rod? The Deep Sea Angler, a rod grows out of the top of her head and hangs in front of her mouth. The tip of her rod glows in the dark, deep waters. Hungry fish see the 'bait' and swim right into her mouth.

Salmon Souffle

Ingredients:
- 2 Tbsp (30 ml) **butter**
- 7 ½ tsp (40 ml) **flour**
- 1 cup (250 ml) **milk**, half and half, **cream**, OR **evaporated milk**
- 1 lb (454 g) canned OR leftover **salmon**, boned, skinned and flaked
- 2 **eggs**, separated
- ¼-½ tsp (1-2 ml) **nutmeg**
- **Salt** and **pepper** to taste

Method:

In a skillet, melt butter. Add flour, stirring until flour is absorbed. Gradually add milk, stirring until well blended, smooth and thick. Add salmon, beaten egg yolks, nutmeg, salt and pepper. Mix well. Beat egg whites until stiff peaks form. Gently fold into salmon mixture. Pour into well buttered souffle dish, bake in a 375°F (190°C) oven for 45 minutes or until souffle has risen. Serve immediately.

Cape Kiwanda Salmon Fritters

Ingredients:
- 1 can (8 oz/225 g) **salmon**, drained and mashed
- 1 large **onion**, minced
- **Salt** and **pepper** to taste
- A few shakes of **vinegar**
- **Butter**
- Sliced **bread**, crusts removed
- 1 **egg**, beaten
- 1 cup (250 ml) **milk**
- 1 cup (250 ml) **flour**
- **Parsley**

Method:

In a small bowl add salmon, onion, salt, pepper and vinegar and mix well. Spread butter on bread. Spread salmon mixture generously between 2 slices of bread as for a sandwich. Make batter by whisking together the egg and milk. Add flour and salt and beat well. Dip each sandwich in the batter and fry in butter until crisp and a golden brown on each side. Garnish with parsley sprigs. Serve while hot.

Salmon Swirls with Cheese Sauce

Ingredients:
- ⅔ cup (150 ml) undiluted **evaporated milk**
- 1 ¼ cups (310 ml) cream of cheese **soup**
- 1 can (8 oz/225 g) **salmon** OR 1 cup (250 ml) leftover, cooked
- ½ cup (125 ml) **celery**, chopped
- 3 Tbsp (45 ml) green **pepper**, chopped
- 2 Tbsp (30 ml) **onion**, finely chopped
- 2 tsp (10 ml) **lemon juice**
- **Salt** and **pepper** to taste
- ⅓ cup (80 ml) undiluted **evaporated milk**
- ⅓ cup (80 ml) **water**
- 2 cups (500 ml) **biscuit mix**

Method:

In a small saucepan blend ⅔ cup (150 ml) evaporated milk with the soup to make a sauce. In a separate bowl, lightly mix ⅓ cup (80 ml) sauce with salmon, celery, green pepper, onion, lemon juice, salt and pepper. Set aside. In a medium size bowl, mix ⅓ cup (80 ml) undiluted evaporated milk, water and biscuit mix with a fork to blend, beating until well blended. On a floured board knead dough gently 8-10 times. Roll into a 16" x 12" (40 x 30 cm) rectangle. Spread with salmon mixture and roll, jelly-roll fashion, beginning at wide side. Seal edges and cut into 8 slices. Place each slice, cut side down, in large buttered muffin tins. Bake in a 425°F (220°C) oven for about 18-20 minutes or until golden brown. When done remove to a serving platter. Heat remaining sauce and pour over swirls. Serves 4.

Baked Salmon Fluff

Ingredients:
- 2 cups (500 ml) **White sauce**, see recipe on page 90
- **Salt**, **pepper**, dry **mustard** and **Worcestershire sauce** to taste
- 2 cups (500 ml) canned **salmon**, flaked
- 4 **egg whites**

Method:
Make a medium white sauce, season with salt, pepper, mustard and Worcestershire sauce. Stir salmon into sauce. Beat egg whites to the stiff peak stage. Gently fold into salmon sauce mixture. Pour into a generously buttered baking dish. Set baking dish into a pan of hot water and cook in a 350°F (180°C) oven for about 45 minutes or until top is puffy.

Salmon Rice Casserole

Ingredients:
- 2 cup (500 ml) white **rice**, cooked and cooled
- 2 **eggs**, beaten
- ⅓ cup (80 ml) **milk**
- 1 Tbsp (15 ml) **butter**, softened
- **Salt** to taste
- **Paprika**
- 1 can (16 oz / 454 g) **salmon**, flaked, bones and skin removed, reserve juice
- **White Sauce**, see recipe on page 90

Method:
Coat a baking dish with non-stick cooking spray. Put a layer of rice in baking dish. Beat together eggs, milk, butter, salt and paprika. Mix in salmon. Spoon the salmon mixture over rice. Spread the remaining rice on top of the salmon. Cover with tin foil. Set baking dish in a larger roasting pan and pour hot water so that it comes half way up the sides of dish. Bake in a 350°F (180°C) oven for 45-60 minutes or until knife inserted in center come out clean. Serve with white sauce. Serves 6.

Salmon in Barbecue Sauce

Ingredients:
- 1 Tbsp (15 ml) **olive oil**
- 1 Tbsp (15 ml) **onion**, minced
- 1 tsp (5 ml) cider **vinegar**
- **Salt** to taste
- 1 Tbsp (15 ml) **Worcestershire sauce**
- 1 can (8 oz / 225 g) **salmon**, flaked and undrained
- ½ cup (125 ml) tomato **catsup**
- 1 Tbsp (15 ml) **butter**
- Few **capers** (optional)
- ½ cup (125 ml) hot **water**
- 1 cup (250 ml) **peas**, cooked

Method:

In a medium size bowl, combine olive oil, onion, cider vinegar, salt and Worcestershire sauce. Stir in salmon. Meanwhile in a heavy sauce pan add catsup, butter, capers and hot water. Stir over low heat until hot. Add salmon mixture and peas to marinade, stir well. Cover and let simmer for 5 minutes. Serve hot over toasted buns. Serves 4.

Chinook Salmon Chops

Ingredients:
- 1 can (1 lb / 454 g) **salmon**, drained and bones crushed
- 4 shredded wheat **biscuits**, crushed
- 2 **eggs**, beaten
- **Salt** and **pepper** to taste
- **Macaroni**
- **Flour**
- **Butter**

Method:

In a bowl, place salmon, wheat biscuits, eggs, salt and pepper and mix well. Shape into rectangular forms resembling chops. Stick a piece of macaroni in the end of each. Dust with flour. Melt butter in large heavy fry pan over medium heat. Fry on both sides until golden brown, about 3 minutes per side.

111

Layered Spaghetti and Salmon Dish

Ingredients:
- ½ lb (225 g) **spaghetti** OR **macaroni**
- ½ lb (225 g) canned **salmon**, flaked, bones mashed, reserve juice
- **Salt** and **pepper** to taste
- **Cheese**, grated
- **Butter** for topping
- 2 **eggs**, beaten
- 2 cups (500 ml) **milk**
- ¼ cup (60 ml) **butter**

Method:
Cook pasta according to package directions. Drain and rinse with cold water. Coat a casserole dish with non-stick cooking spray. Layer pasta, salmon, salt, pepper, cheese, topping each layer with butter, until pasta and salmon are all used. Beat together eggs, milk, ¼ cup (60 ml) butter and reserved juice from salmon. Pour this mixture over the pasta and salmon. Sprinkle with more grated cheese. Bake in a 350°F (180°C) oven until casserole is cooked through, bubbly and golden, about 25-30 minutes.

Caviar Scrambled Eggs

Ingredients:
- 18 **eggs**
- **Salt** and **pepper** to taste
- ¼ cup (60 ml) **butter**
- ⅓ cup (80 ml) **whipping cream**
- ¼ cup (60 ml) **parsley**, chopped (optional)
- ¼ cup (60 ml) **salmon*** **caviar**

Method:
Whisk eggs, salt and pepper in a bowl. Over medium heat, melt butter in a heavy skillet. Cook eggs, stirring constantly until at the creamy stage. Do not over cook. Stir in cream and parsley if using. Cook until eggs are set, but still moist. Place eggs on a warm serving platter. Form a hollow in top; spoon in caviar. Serves 12.

*Golden caviar may be substituted.

SEAFOOD

s Baked Salmon 84

Creamed
Salmon on
Toast 89

Creamy Pasta & Salmon Salad 94

Jellied Salmon Mold 115

Altoona Salmon and Corn Pie

Ingredients:
- ¼ cup (60 ml) **butter**, melted
- ¼ cup (60 ml) **onion**, chopped
- ¼ cup (60 ml) **celery**, chopped
- ¼ cup (60 ml) green **pepper**, chopped
- ¼ cup (60 ml) **flour**
- 2 cups (500 ml) **milk**
- 2 **tomatoes**, coarsely chopped
- 1 ½ cups (375 ml) canned kernel **corn**
- 2 cans (7 ½ oz / 213 g each) **salmon**, mashed bones, flaked
- **Salt** and **pepper** to taste
- **Pastry** to cover top of casserole

Method:

Melt butter in a large heavy fry pan. Saute onion, celery and green pepper until tender. Stir in flour, cook 2-3 minutes until absorbed. Slowly blend in milk, stirring until smooth, thickened and boiling. Add tomatoes, corn and salmon, heat through. Season with salt and pepper. Pour mixture into casserole dish which has been coated with non-stick cooking spray. Cover dish with pastry. With sharp knife, make vents so steam is able to escape. Bake in a 375°F (190°C) oven for 15 -20 minutes or until mixture is bubbly and crust is golden brown.

Fresh fish does not have a "fishy" odor, but may have an ocean-like smell.

Salmon Croquettes

Ingredients:
1 can (1 lb / 454 g) **salmon**, drain, mash bones, flake
½ cup (250 ml) soft **bread crumbs**
1 cup (250 ml) thick **white sauce** see **White Sauce** recipe on page 90.
Salt, pepper and **cayenne** to taste
1 Tbsp (15 ml) **onion**, minced
2 tsp (10 ml) **lemon juice**
1 cup (250 ml) **Westcoaster Shakin' Bake Mix**, recipe follows
2 **eggs**, beaten

Method:
In a bowl combine salmon, soft bread crumbs, white sauce, seasonings, onion and lemon juice. Cover, place in refrigerator for 1 hour. With floured hands, shape about ¼ cup (60 ml) of chilled mixture into croquettes. Roll in dried bread crumbs, then beaten egg and again in dried crumbs. Deep-fry in hot oil (350°F / 180°C) for 3-5 minutes or until a golden brown color. Drain on paper towel. Serve with Cucumber Sauce, see recipe on page 47. Serves 6.

Westcoaster Shakin' Bake Mix

Ingredients:
2 Tbsp (30 ml) **marjoram**
2 Tbsp (30 ml) **dill weed**
2 Tbsp (30 ml) **parsley flakes**
2 Tbsp (30 ml) **sage**
2 Tbsp (30 ml) **thyme**
1 Tbsp (15 ml) **lemon pepper**
1 Tbsp (15 ml) **basil**
1 tsp (5 ml) **onion powder**
½ tsp (2 ml) **chili powder** (optional)
Dried **bread crumbs**, finely crushed

Method:
In a bowl thoroughly combine all spices. Store in air-tight container. For each ½ cup (125 ml) of bread crumbs, stir in 1 Tbsp (15 ml) of seafood mix.

Jellied Salmon Mold

Contributed by Dawn Bolton, Edmonds, Washington, USA

Ingredients:

1 can (8 oz / 225 g) canned **salmon** or leftover cooked **salmon**, drained, flaked, bones mashed

¼ cup (60 ml) **vinegar**

Salt to taste

Dash **paprika**

1 pkg of **gelatin**

½ cup (125 ml) **milk**, cold, divided

2 **eggs**, hard-cooked

9 large pitted **olive**s, coarsely ground

1 sweet **pickle** OR 1 Tbsp (15 ml) sweet green **relish**

2 Tbsp (30 ml) **chili sauce**

½ cup (125 ml) **salad dressing** (Miracle Whip OR **Mayonnaise**), divided

Long English **cucumber**

Olives

Pimento

Lettuce leaves

Method:

In a medium size bowl, combine salmon, vinegar, salt, paprika and rub smooth using the back of a wooden spoon, set aside. In a separate bowl, grind together eggs, pickle, olives, chili sauce and ¼ cup (60 ml) of the salad dressing, blend into salmon mixture. In a small bowl, sprinkle gelatin on ¼ cup (60 ml) of cold milk for 5 minutes, do not stir. In a small sauce pan, heat remaining milk but do not boil. Add gelatin mixture and heat 2-3 minutes, stirring until completely dissolved but do not boil this mixture. Add remaining salad dressing, stirring until smooth. Combine with salmon ingredients and mix well. Pour into a fish mold or individual molds and place in refrigerator until set approximately 4 hours. Unmold salad by lowering the base of the mold into warm water to loosen contents. Leave for only 10 seconds (no longer or the gelatin salad may begin to melt). Invert on a platter. Decorate with cucumber, olives, pimento, lemon slices and lettuce, if desired.

Scallops

The small "Pink" or "swimming" scallops found on the West Coast are delicious. Most people eat only the large single muscle, which is a shame, because the red roe and ivory milt of scallops are also very good to eat when cooked. Scallops are best when very lightly cooked and in fact are good raw on the half shell.

Pinks are best steamed for 2 -3 minutes, the larger Bays and Seas scallops should be cooked for 3-4 minutes. No scallop will take longer than 6-8 minutes to cook. Cook only until scallop turns opaque and feels firm. Do not over-cook as this will toughen the scallop. They can be used in recipes in the same way as clams, mussels, or crab.

To shuck scallops, open the shell with a knife and scoop out the muscle and roe, if any. Throw away the dark-colored innards and the little crescent-shaped muscle on the side as this part is very tough to eat. Rinse under cold running water to remove any sand from crevices, pat dry with paper towels.

Because scallops perish quickly out of water, they're usually sold shucked. All fresh scallops should have a sweet smell and a fresh, moist sheen. They should be refrigerated immediately after purchased and used within a day or two at the most.

Coquilles St. Jacques

Ingredients:

3 Tbsp (45 ml) **butter**, melted, divided

¾ cup (175 ml) fresh **bread crumbs**

2 Tbsp (30 ml) **parsley**, minced

¼ tsp (1 ml) **thyme**

¼ tsp (1 ml) **nutmeg** (optional)

Salt and **pepper** to taste

6 **shallots**, finely chopped

¼ lb (125 g) **mushrooms**, sliced

¼ cup (60 ml) dry white **wine**

1 cup (250 ml) half-and-half **cream**

12 fresh **scallops**, cut into quarters

½ cup (250 ml) **dried bread crumbs**, finely crushed

¾ cup (175 ml) Swiss **cheese**, grated

Rock **salt**

Method:

In a small bowl, combine 2 Tbsp (30 ml) melted butter, fresh bread crumbs, parsley, thyme, nutmeg, salt and pepper till crumbly, set aside. Place the remaining 1 Tbsp (15 ml) butter in a large hot fry pan and add shallots and cook for about 2 minutes, until softened but not browned. Stir in mushrooms and cook 5 minutes longer until mushrooms are softened. Add wine and increase heat to a simmer or until wine has almost evaporated, about 3 minutes. Stir in cream and boil until thickened. Add scallops and cook until they are opaque, about 2-3 minutes. Place shells on cookie sheet surrounded by rock salt or crumbled tin foil. Spoon scallop mixture between four scallop shells and sprinkle with crumbs and cheese. Place under broiler until golden brown and cheese is bubbly, about 2-3 minutes. Caution: Shells become very hot!

Hot Scallop & Spinach Luncheon Salad

Ingredients:

- 7 oz (200 g) fresh **spinach** leaves, washed and stemmed
- 4 oz (115 g) Blue **cheese**, Gorgonzola OR Feta **cheese**, crumbled
- 1 lb (454 g) fresh **scallops***, cut in half if large
- 2 tsp (10 ml) **olive oil**
- ½ cup (125 ml) Italian-style **dressing**
- ½ cup (125 ml) **peanuts**, coarsely chopped

Method:

Arrange spinach leaves on 4 serving plates. Crumble cheese over leaves. Rinse scallops under running water and pat dry. If scallops are large, cut in half horizontally. In a large fry pan, over high heat, bring oil to frying temperature. When hot add half of the scallops and cook, stirring often and turning over until opaque through to center (cut to see if done), about 1-2 minutes depending on the size. Remove scallops from pan; set aside. Cook remaining scallops in the same way adding more oil if needed. Heat dressing to a simmer. Arrange scallops over spinach and cheese, drizzle with hot Italian dressing then sprinkle with peanuts. Serves 4.

*You can use, instead of the scallops, crab, shrimp or salmon.

Bear Cove Grilled Scallops

Ingredients:
- 3 Tbsp (45 ml) **lemon juice**
- 2 Tbsp (30 ml) salad **oil**
- 1 Tbsp (15 ml) **honey**
- 1 Tbsp (15 ml) **soy sauce**
- ¼ tsp (1 ml) ground **ginger**
- 1 small **clove garlic**, minced
- 1 lb (454 g) fresh **scallops**, cut in bite size pieces
- ¼ cup (60 ml) **sesame seeds**, toasted

Method:

Combine lemon juice, oil, honey, soy sauce, ginger and garlic in a bowl. Add scallops and toss until well coated. Cover bowl with plastic wrap and marinate 3 hours in refrigerator, turning scallops at half time. Stir frequently. Remove scallops from marinade. Set marinade aside. Dividing evenly, place scallops on either metal or wooden skewers which have been soaked first in water for 20 minutes. When ready to cook, oil hot grate with a paper towel dipped in vegetable oil or spray grate well. Place skewered scallops on hot grate and broil about 3 inches (7.5 cm) from heat source, turning occasionally and basting with marinade. Scallops are done when opaque throughout and feel firm but not hard, about 2-3 minutes per side. Spread sesame seeds on waxed paper. Turn each skewer of scallops through the seeds to coat evenly. Serve while hot. Serves 4.

Shrimp

Shrimp, on the West Coast, vary in size from 1-3 inches (2.5-7.5 cm). Large shrimp have been loosely called prawns but prawns are an entirely different species from shrimp. Prawns are caught differently and live in different areas. A prawn is related to the lobster family.

Shrimp cook quickly, are sweet, tender-crisp, delicate and low in calories. They are marketed fresh, frozen, shelled, cooked and canned. Raw shrimp are called "green" although they are gray in color and the texture is more like that of a jellyfish and are translucent. You will know if shrimp are cooked by their color. When cooked, the shells will be a pink color and the meat snowy white. You don't usually buy them raw out of the shell. Shrimp are sold with their heads removed. They should be eaten the same day as purchased or may be frozen up to 3 months in an air-tight container.

To prepare shrimp for cooking without the shell, very little needs to be done. If you have purchased them in the shell you will need to remove the shell and sand vein. To shell the shrimp, first remove the legs. Second, starting at the head end of the shrimp, gently open the shell down the belly. When you reach the tail section, cut the body section of shell off leaving the tail shell in place. To remove the sand vein that runs along the back of the shrimp, insert a skewer or round toothpick under the vein and gently tease out. This is called deveining.

Shrimp may be cooked in or out of the shell. Immerse shrimp in boiling salted water (2 Tbsp/30 ml salt to each qt/l water). Add shrimp. Small shrimp should be cooked for 2-3 minutes and the large prawn for up to 5 minutes. The whole shell turns pink. The meat of the shrimp turns bright white (with little pink veins). Be careful not to overcook shrimp and prawns. Drain and use shrimp hot or cover and chill. If the shrimp were cooked in the shell, remove shell and sand vein. Removing the sand vein in small shrimp is only for cosmetic reasons or personal preference. If you have a large shrimp, it is best to devein it as the intestinal vein contains grit.

Oriental Shrimp Stir-fry

Ingredients:

- ⅔ cup (160 ml) **soy sauce**
- 1 cup (250 ml) **orange juice**, cold
- 2 Tbsp (15 ml) **corn starch**
- 1 pkg (8 oz / 227 g) steamed fried **noodles**
- ¼ cup (60 ml) vegetable **oil**
- 6 green **onions**, julienned
- 3 small **cloves garlic**, minced
- 3 Tbsp (15 ml) fresh **ginger**, peeled and thinly sliced
- 4 large **carrots**, cut into matchsticks
- 2 cups (500 ml) fresh **mushrooms**, sliced
- 1 large sweet red **pepper**, cut in strips
- ½ lb (225 g) Sugar or Snow **peas**, trimmed
- 2 Tbsp (30 ml) vegetable **oil**
- 1 lb (454 g) medium **shrimp**, cooked

Method:

Combine soy sauce, orange juice and corn starch in a small jar with lid. Set aside. Prepare noodles according to package directions, drain well and keep warm. Heat wok or large skillet over high heat, add ¼ cup (60 ml) vegetable oil, mix in onions, garlic and ginger, stir-fry for about 30 seconds. Add carrots and stir-fry 4 minutes uncovered. Mix in mushrooms, red pepper and peas and stir-fry 2 minutes. Blend in corn starch mixture and cook and stir until thickened and bubbly. If desired, cover and steam vegetables being careful not to scorch bottom. Remove vegetables from wok and place in warmed casserole dish. Meanwhile, add 2 Tbsp (30 ml) vegetable oil and shrimp to wok and stir-fry shrimp 2-3 minutes until heated through. Add to vegetables and serve over noodles. Serves 6.

Shrimp & Rice Casserole

Contributed by Gladys Lancaster, Abbotsford, B.C., Canada

Ingredients:
2 cups (500 ml) cooked
  rice
1 can (6 ½ oz / 175 ml)
  broken **shrimp**
Salt and **pepper** to taste
1 cup (250 ml) **White
  Sauce** see recipe on
  page 90.

Method:
In a medium-size bowl, mix
all ingredients. Place in a
greased casserole dish and bake
at 350°F (180°C) for about 20-25
minutes until bubbly and nicely
browned.

The Shrimp of Hearts

Contributed by Josie Chinnery, Clayburn, B.C., Canada

Ingredients:
2 ½ cups (625 ml)
  mushrooms, sliced
¼ cup (60 ml) **butter**
5 Tbsp (75 ml) **flour**
½ cup (125 ml) **milk**
2 cups (500 ml) **light cream**
½ tsp (2 ml) **salt**
½ tsp (2 ml) **Worcestershire**
Few drops **Tabasco**
2 Tbsp (30 ml) **onion**,
  minced
2 Tbsp (30 ml) **parsley**,
  chopped
2 cans (1 lb / 454 g) ea
  artichoke hearts, drained
2 lbs (1 kg) **shrimp**, cooked
½ cup (125 ml) Gruyere
  cheese, grated

Method:
In a large heavy fry pan,
sauté mushrooms in butter for
5 minutes. Add flour and stir
for 3 minutes. Gradually stir in
milk, cream, salt,
Worcestershire sauce, Tabasco,
onion and parsley. Cook over
moderate heat, stirring
constantly until thickened and
smooth. Remove from heat. In a
greased shallow dish, arrange
the artichoke hearts; place
shrimp over hearts. Pour
mushroom sauce over the
shrimp and sprinkle with
cheese. Bake, uncovered in a
moderate oven for about 20
minutes until cooked and
bubbly.

Shrimp and Macaroni Salad

Contributed by Hazel Campbell, Abbotsford, B.C., Canada

Ingredients:
1 cup (250 ml) petite
  macaroni
1 can (7 oz / 199 ml) **shrimp**
1 cup (250 ml) **celery**,
  chopped
1 **onion**, diced
¼ cup (60 ml) green **pepper**,
  diced
2 hard-boiled **eggs**, chopped
1 cup (250 ml) **mayonnaise**
¼ cup (60 ml) French
  dressing
¼ cup (60 ml) **pimento**,
  diced
Salt to taste

Method:
Cook macaroni according to package directions. Drain, rinse and cool. Drain shrimp. Mix all ingredients together in a glass bowl, cover and chill.

Mukilteo Curried Shrimp

Ingredients:
1 Tbsp (15 ml) **butter**
1 small **onion**, chopped
1 small carton **sour cream**
1 cup (250 ml) cream of
  mushroom **soup**,
  undiluted
2 tsp / 10 ml (or to taste)
  curry powder
½ lb (225 g) **shrimp**,
  cooked

Method:
In a heavy cast iron fry pan over medium heat, melt butter, sauté onions until translucent. Combine remaining ingredients except the shrimp, with the onions in top of double boiler. Heat until mixture bubbles, add shrimp and heat through. Serve over hot rice. Serves 4.

Quick Shrimp Curry

Ingredients:
- ½ cup (125 ml) **onion**, minced
- 2 Tbsp (30 ml) **olive oil**
- 1 Tbsp (15 ml) **flour**
- 2 tsp (10 ml) **curry powder**
- 1 cup (250 ml) **chicken stock**
- 1 ½ lbs (750 g) medium fresh **shrimp**, cooked peeled and deveined
- 2 Tbsp (30 ml) **parsley** OR **cilantro**, minced
- **Salt** and **pepper** to taste
- ¼ cup (60 ml) toasted **coconut** OR plumped **raisins** (optional)

Method:
Sauté onion in hot oil until just softened, about 2-3 minutes. Sprinkle flour and curry over onions. Cook, while stirring until onions are fully coated. Cook for an additional 2-3 minutes. Slowly add the stock, stirring until boiling and thickened. Add shrimp, heat through. Stir in parsley, salt and pepper. Serve curry sauce over rice and sprinkle with coconut or raisins. Serves 4.

Shrimp Tempura

Ingredients:
- 1 cup (250 ml) cake OR tempura **flour**
- ¼ tsp (1 ml) **salt**
- ¼ tsp (1 ml) **baking soda**
- 1 **egg**, slightly beaten
- 1 ¼ cups (310 ml) ice cold **water**
- 2 Tbsp (30 ml) **soy sauce**
- **Oil** for deep frying
- 1 lb (454 g) fresh large **shrimp**, peeled, deveined and tails on

Method:
In a bowl, combine flour, salt and baking soda. In a small bowl, beat egg slightly, add water and soy sauce. Mix wet ingredients into dry ingredients, batter should be lumpy. Dip shrimp into batter, leaving tail uncoated. Heat about 2 inches (5 cm) of oil in a wok over high heat to 375°F (190°C). Add a few shrimp at a time, deep fry for 2-3 minutes, turning once, or until batter turns lightly golden in color and puffy. Shrimp should be white when cooked. Serve with Lemon Sauce, see recipe on page 11.

Shrimp Green Salad with Olives

Ingredients:

- 1 lb (454 g) medium-large fresh **shrimp**, about 20
- 1 Tbsp (15 ml) plus 2 tsp (10 ml) **lemon juice**
- **Salt** and **pepper** to taste
- ¼ cup (60 ml) **olive oil**
- 1 head green-leaf **lettuce**, about 8 cups (2 l) torn, leaves OR use **spinach** instead
- 2 hard-boiled **eggs**, peeled and quartered
- ½ cup (125 ml) green **olives**, chopped
- ½ cup (125 ml) black **olives**, chopped
- 2 Tbsp (30 ml) **pimento**, chopped
- 2 Tbsp (30 ml) **parsley**, chopped
- ½ tsp (2 ml) fresh **garlic**, minced

Method:

In a large pot of boiling water, cook raw shrimp for about 3-4 minutes or until done, the whole shell turns pink but the meat of the shrimp turns bright white (with little pink veins). Drain. When cooled, peel and chill. In a small jar, combine lemon juice, salt and pepper, shake until salt dissolves. Add olive oil and shake again to mix well, set aside. Just before serving, in a large bowl combine lettuce with the eggs and shrimp. In a small bowl, combine olives, pimento, parsley and garlic and toss with the lettuce. Pour the dressing over and lightly toss. Serves 4.

"Fish in the summer and fun in the winter." Everything in its place.

"You are making a nice kettle of fish." Making a mess of affairs.

"You are like a fish out of water." Not at home in your environment.

Thai Shrimp with Sesame Noodles

Ingredients:
- 1 lb (454 g) fresh **shrimp**, peeled and deveined
- 1 bottle (8 oz / 227 ml) light **Italian dressing**
- 2 Tbsp (30 ml) chunky **peanut butter**
- 1 Tbsp (15 ml) **soy sauce**
- 1 Tbsp (15 ml) **honey**
- 1 tsp (5 ml) **ginger**, peeled and grated
- ½ tsp (2 ml) crushed red **pepper** flakes
- 1 pkg (8 oz / 225 g) angel hair or capellini **pasta**
- 2 Tbsp (30 ml) light flavored salad **oil**
- 1 Tbsp (15 ml) sesame **oil**
- 1 medium **carrot**, shredded
- 1 cup (250 ml) green **onion**, chopped
- 2 Tbsp (30 ml) **cilantro** leaves, fresh, chopped
- Few **cilantro** sprigs for garnish

Method:
Marinate shrimp for 1 ½ hours in ⅓ cup (80 ml) of Italian dressing in a glass dish, stirring occasionally. Cover and refrigerate. In a small bowl, mix peanut butter, soy sauce, honey, ginger, red pepper and remaining dressing until well blended. Set aside. When shrimp have been marinating for 1 hour; cook pasta per package directions, drain and keep warm. While pasta is cooking, heat salad oil and sesame oil in a large saucepan or wok until very hot. Cook carrot for 1 minute. Drain off salad dressing from shrimp. Add green onion and shrimp to carrots and stir constantly. Cook until shrimp turn white, about 2-3 minutes. Toss pasta, sauce mixture, shrimp mixture and cilantro together in a large bowl. Garnish with sprigs of cilantro and serve. This is a nice main dish meal for 4.

Barbecue Garlic Shrimp

Ingredients:

4-6 **garlic cloves**, pressed
¼ cup (60 ml) **lemon juice**
¼ cup (60 ml) **olive oil**
½ tsp (2 ml) coarsely ground black **pepper**
½ tsp (2 ml) cayenne **pepper** (optional)
½ tsp (2 ml) coarse **salt**
1 ¼ lbs. (569 g) large fresh **shrimp**, peeled and deveined, leave tails on
Lemon wedges, **parsley** spring, **garlic bread**, if desired

Method:

Combine and stir garlic, lemon juice, olive oil, peppers and salt in a small bowl. Thread shrimp on a double-pronged skewer (or if wooden skewers, let soak 20 minutes in water). Lay skewers in flat dish, large enough to hold them. Pour marinade over shrimp. Cover and marinade for 20 minutes in refrigerator, turning once. Remove skewers from marinade reserving mixture. Have grill preheated and well oiled, lay skewers on top of grate and grill until the shrimp are white, about 2-3 minutes per side, turning skewers and basting shrimp with remaining marinade. Serve with lemon wedges, a sprig of parsley and garlic bread, if desired.

Two fathers and two sons go fishing and catch three large fish together. Yet, each one has a whole fish to himself. How can this be true?

Answer: The three are grandfather, father and son.

Westcoast Butterfly Shrimp

Ingredients:
2 lbs (1 kg) medium to
large fresh **shrimp**,
peeled and deveined,
tails left on
2 **eggs**, separated
¾ cup (175 ml) **beer**
1 Tbsp (15 ml) **olive oil**
1 cup (250 ml) sifted **flour**
Flour for dipping
Soy sauce
Mustard Sauce

Method:
Pat shrimp dry. Slit shrimp
down the center back, starting
about ¼ inch (.5 cm) from tail,
without separating the halves.
Press shrimp flat to make
butterflies. In a medium-size
bowl, beat together egg yolks,
beer, olive oil and flour. Beat
egg whites until stiff. Fold into
batter. Dip shrimp into flour
then into batter. Deep-fry a few
at a time in hot oil 365°F
(185°C) until golden brown,
about 2-3 minutes. Shrimp meat
should be white when cooked.
Remove from oil and drain on
absorbent paper towel. Serve
shrimp while hot with soy
sauce and Mustard Sauce, see
recipe on page 11.

*Refrigerate your catch promptly and
keep it cold. Frozen seafood should be
solidly frozen and wrapped tightly.
Avoid products with ice-crystals. Never
buy precooked food that has been
displayed alongside raw fish. Bacteria
from raw fish can contaminate cooked
seafood.*

Shrimp and Artichoke Pasta

Ingredients:
- 2 Tbsp (30 ml) **olive oil**
- 1 lb (454 g) large fresh **shrimp**, peeled and deveined
- 2 tsp (10 ml) **garlic**, minced , divided
- **Salt** and **pepper** to taste
- 1 ½ cups (375 ml) chicken **broth**
- 8 oz (225 g) fresh plum **tomatoes**, coarsely chopped
- 1 box (9 oz / 255 g) frozen **artichoke** hearts, quartered
- 2 Tbsp (30 ml) **butter** OR **margarine**
- ½ cup (125 ml) **parsley**, chopped
- 1 lb (454 g) **linguine**, cooked and drained

Method:

In a large skillet, heat oil. Add shrimp and 1 tsp (5 ml) garlic. Cook over medium heat for 2 minutes or until shrimp turn opaque. Stir often. With a slotted spoon remove shrimp to a bowl and set aside. Into the skillet stir remaining garlic, salt, pepper, and broth. Bring to a boil and cook to reduce liquid slightly, about 3-5 minutes. Add tomatoes and artichokes, stir and cook 5-7 minutes until artichoke hearts are tender. Add shrimp to the artichoke mixture and cook about 2 minutes or until shrimp are cooked completely through and mixture is hot. Shrimp meat should be white when cooked. Remove from heat and stir in butter and parsley. To serve pour over hot pasta and toss to mix. Serves 8.

Shrimp Kebabs

Ingredients:
- 1 lb (454 g) large fresh **shrimp**, shelled and deveined
- 1 medium-size **onion**, cut in quarters, then sliced in half through widest section
- 1 large red **pepper**, cut in 1 inch (2.5 cm) squares, then into triangles
- 1 large yellow **pepper**, cut in 1 inch (2.5 cm) squares, then into triangles
- ½ cup (125 ml) herb style **dressing**
- Crushed red **pepper** flakes, to taste

Dip

Ingredients:
- ½ cup (125 ml) Ranch style **dressing**
- ¼ cup (60 ml) **chutney**
- 1 Tbsp (15 ml) **honey**
- 1 tsp (5 ml) **curry powder**
- 2-3 drops **Tabasco sauce**

Method:
Place shrimp on skewers (if using wooden skewers, soak first in water for 20 minutes), alternating them with onion and pepper pieces. Mix dressing with red pepper flakes. Lay skewers in an oblong glass dish, pour marinade over and let season for 30 minutes, covered, in the refrigerator, turning skewers at half time. Drain kebabs and cook on preheated well oiled grill (or broil) for 2-3 minutes per side, turning once. Baste frequently with dressing as shrimp tend to dry out. When shrimp turn white, they are cooked. Discard marinade. In a small bowl combine dip ingredients. Refrigerate until ready to use. Serve kebabs with dip and grilled garlic bread.

Shrimp with Curry Sauce

Contributed by LeAnne Bowden, Ladysmith, B.C., Canada

Ingredients:

- ¼ cup (60 ml) **butter** OR **margarine**
- ¼ cup (60 ml) **flour**
- 2 cups (500 ml) **chicken stock**
- 1 tsp (5 ml) **curry powder**
- **Salt** and **pepper** to taste
- 1 cup (250 ml) **shrimp**, cooked

Method:

Melt margarine in heavy fry pan over medium heat. Add flour, stir until absorbed, cook 2-3 minutes. Remove pan from heat, slowly stir in chicken stock. Return pan to heat, stir, cook until thickened and smooth. Add curry powder, salt and pepper to taste. Simmer for about 10 minutes. Add shrimp and heat through. Serve over rice.

Shrimp Luncheon Dish

Contributed by Shirley Copeland, Mission, B.C., Canada

Ingredients:

- 1 ½ cups (375 ml) **onions**, chopped
- 1 ½ cups (375 ml) **celery**, chopped
- ½ cup (125 ml) **butter**
- 2 cups (500 ml) **applesauce**
- 3 cans **celery** soup
- 1 can **mushrooms**, drained
- ¼ tsp (1 ml) **salt**
- **Curry** to taste (2 tsp-2 Tbsp) (10 ml-30 ml)
- 2 lbs (1 kg) **shrimp**, cooked

Method:

In a large pot, cook onions and celery in butter. Stir in next 5 ingredients and simmer gently for 15 minutes uncovered. Add shrimp and heat through. Do not boil as this toughens the shrimp. Serves 12.

Baked Shrimp Salad Supreme

Ingredients:
- 1 cup (250 ml) **mayonnaise**
- 1 Tbsp (15 ml) prepared **mustard**
- 1 Tbsp (15 ml) **parsley**, chopped
- 1 Tbsp (15 ml) green **onions**, sliced
- 2 cups (500 ml) **shrimp**, cooked and cut in half
- ½ cup (125 ml) whole **almonds**
- 1 cup (250 ml) **celery**, finely chopped
- ¼ **pimento**, chopped
- 1 can (8 oz/225 ml) crushed **pineapple**, drained
- 1 ½ cups (375 ml) herb-seasoned **croutons**
- **Paprika** to taste

Method:

Mix mayonnaise, mustard, parsley and onions together in a large bowl. Stir in shrimp, almonds, celery, pimento and pineapple. Coat a 6" x 10" (15 x 25 cm) baking dish with non-stick cooking spray. Place shrimp mixture in dish and top with croutons. Bake in a 350°F (180°C) oven for 20-30 minutes or until mixture is bubbly. Just before serving, turn croutons into hot shrimp mixture and sprinkle with paprika.
Serve 6-8.

Did you hear about the want ad for a female partner? Gentleman looking for spouse. Must like the outdoors, would not mind digging for worms, cleaning the day's catch and cooking same. Most important, she must own a boat. Any lady interested in a relationship, please send me a picture of the boat!

Polynesian Salad

Contributed by Barb Hood, Ashcroft, B.C., Canada

Salad

Ingredients:
- 1 ½ cups (375 ml) cooked **rice**
- 1 ½ cups (375 ml) **celery**, diced
- ½ cup (125 ml) green **onion**s, chopped
- ½ cup (125 ml) green **pepper**, chopped
- ½ cup (125 ml) frozen **peas**, thawed
- 1-2 cups (250-500 ml) **shrimp**, cooked
- 5 oz / 140 g (approx.) Chow mein **noodles**

Method:

Combine all salad ingredients except noodles in a large glass bowl. In a separate bowl, mix together dressing ingredients and pour over salad. At serving time mix in chow mein noodles. Sprinkle some on top.

Dressing

Ingredients:
- ½ cup (125 m) salad **oil**
- 3 Tbsp (45 ml) **vinegar**
- 2 tsp (10 ml) **sugar**
- ½ tsp (2 ml) **salt**
- ½ tsp (2 ml) **celery salt**
- 1-2 tsp (5-10 ml) **curry powder**
- 2 Tbsp (30 ml) **soy sauce**

Smelt

Smelt are a small fish, generally not bigger than 12 inches (30 cm) in length. They have a high oil content which was highly prized by native Indians, not just as food, but also for barter. For a real treat try cooking smelt on a beach fire right after collecting them. Fry them, with or without head, gutted or not, in butter and eat them like corn-on-the-cob, nibbling around the bone.

Smelt are a soft, oily but mild, sweet-tasting flavored fish. The bones are soft and edible, and soften even more when cooked.

How to tell if smelt is cooked? Follow our recipes but just before the allotted time check to see: Smelt should be opaque and should also flake into chunks when fork-tested in the thickest portion of the fish, yet still be moist looking not dried out.

To clean smelt, spread open the outter gills. With your finger take hold of the inner gills and pull gently. The parts unfit for eating are all attached to the inner gills and come away together, leaving the smelt in perfect shape. Rinse fish under cold running water and pat dry. Keep refrigerated until ready to use.

Pan Fried Smelt

Ingredients:
- ½ cup (125 ml) **cornmeal**
- ½ cup (125 ml) **flour**
- 1 Tbsp (15 ml) **salt**
- ½ tsp (2 ml) **pepper**
- 2 lbs (1 kg) **smelt**, cleaned
- **Oil** for frying

Method:
Mix cornmeal, flour, salt and pepper together in a shallow dish. Dip smelt in water, then roll into cornmeal mixture. Fry in hot oil about 4-5 minutes on each side or until nicely browned. The smelt should be opaque and flake into chunks when fork-tested. Serves 4.

Finnish Sauced Smelt

Ingredients:
- 1 ½ cups (375 ml) **water**
- 1 ½ lbs (750 g) **smelt**, cleaned
- **Salt** to taste
- Dash of **pepper**
- Cheddar **cheese**, grated

Method:
Place water in a large pan, simmer smelt for 2-4 minutes to make a stock. Remove smelt and reserve stock. Lay smelt in a single layer in a greased baking dish. Pour sauce (recipe follows) over the top, sprinkle with salt, pepper and grated cheese. Bake in a 350°F (180°C) oven for 15 minutes or until golden and bubbly. The smelt should be opaque and flake into chunks when fork-tested.

Sauce

Ingredients:
- 2 Tbsp (30 ml) **butter**
- 1 Tbsp (15 ml) **flour**
- 2 **egg yolks**, slightly beaten
- 1 cup (250 ml) reserved **fish stock**

Method:
Melt butter over low heat in a medium-size saucepan. Remove saucepan from heat, gradually stir in flour and egg yolks to make a smooth paste. Return to heat. Gradually add fish stock, stirring until thickened and smooth.

Broiled Smelt

Ingredients:
  Butter, melted
  Lemon juice
  Smelt, cleaned

Method:
  In a small bowl, combine melted butter and lemon juice. Brush smelt with butter mixture. Place in a greased pan and broil about 4 inch (10 cm) from heat source for 5-6 minutes per side or until nicely browned. The smelt should be opaque and flake into chunks when fork-tested. Serve with Mustard Sauce, see recipe on page 11.

Italian-Style Smelt

Ingredients:
  2 lbs (1 kg) **smelt**, cleaned
  1 cup (250 ml) spaghetti **sauce** with mushrooms
  ½ tsp (2 ml) **oregano**
  ¼ cup (60 ml) Mozzarella **cheese**, shredded

Method:
  Coat a baking dish with non-stick cooking spray. Lay smelt in a single layer in dish. Blend spaghetti sauce and oregano; pour over fish. Sprinkle cheese over the top and bake in a 400°F (200°C) oven for 12-15 minutes. The smelt should be opaque and flake into chunks when fork-tested. Serves 4-6.

Paté of Smelt

Ingredients:
- 2 pkgs (8 oz/225 g ea) **cream cheese**, softened
- 2 tsp (10 ml) **horseradish**
- 3 Tbsp (45 ml) **lemon juice**
- 2 Tbsp (30 ml) **onion**, grated
- 1 cup (250 ml) cooked **smelt**, cleaned, boned and mashed
- ½ cup (125 ml) **potato chips**, crushed
- 2 Tbsp (30 ml) **parsley**, chopped

Method:
In a medium-size bowl, cream together the cheese, seasonings and smelt. Mix well. Shape into a mound, roll in combined potato chips and parsley. Place on a serving plate with assorted crackers.

Au Gratin Smelt

Ingredients:
- 6 slices **toast**, buttered, crusts removed
- 2 lbs (1 kg) **smelt**, cleaned, fried, bones and fins removed
- 2 **eggs**, slightly beaten
- ½ cup (125 ml) **milk**
- 1 tsp (5 ml) Dijon-style **mustard**
- ½ tsp (2 ml) **paprika**
- **Salt** and **pepper** to taste
- 1 cup (250 ml) Cheddar **cheese**, grated

Method:
Butter a baking dish and lay half the toast in the bottom. Cover with fried smelt and add another layer of toast. Mix eggs, milk, mustard, paprika, salt and pepper together and pour over toast. Sprinkle with cheese. Place dish in a larger pan. Pour hot water to come halfway up the sides of dish. Bake for 45-60 minutes in a 350°F (180°C) oven. Serves 6.

Red Snapper

Red Snapper? The fish we buy as Pacific Red Snapper is often called Rockfish or Rock Cod. We will call them snapper in our recipes. Rockfish are a large group of medium-size bony-cheeked fish found all along our West Coast. Rockfish are firm fleshed and delicious. The white meat of Rockfish is low in fat. A very versatile fish that can be cooked in many ways as you can see by our recipes. How can you tell when Rockfish are cooked: it should be opaque and should also flake into chunks when fork-tested in the thickest portion of the fish, yet still be moist looking, not dried out.

Henry's son, David, burst into the house, crying. His mother asked him what the problem was. "Daddy and I were fishing, and he hooked a giant fish. Really big. Then, while he was reeling it in, the line busted and the fish got away." "Now come on, David," his mother said, "a big boy like you shouldn't be crying about an accident like that. You should have just laughed it off." "But that's just what I did, mommy."

Barbecued Snapper
with Orange Butter

Ingredients:

1 whole **Red Snapper**
(about 2 ½ lbs/1.2 kg)
dressed with head and
tail left on
⅓ cup (80 ml) salad **oil**
2 Tbsp (30 ml) **fennel
seeds**, crushed
2 Tbsp (30 ml) dry **sherry**
1 tsp (5 ml) **salt** or to taste
1 Tbsp (15 ml) fresh **sage**,
minced
1 Tbsp (15 ml) fresh
parsley, minced
6 Tbsp (90 ml) **butter** OR
margarine
2 Tbsp (30 ml) **orange
juice**
¾ tsp (4 ml) **sugar**
Few sprigs **sage** and
parsley for garnish

Method:

Prepare barbecue grill. Rinse
fish under running water and
cut 4 slashes in the thick part of
the fish on each side. Pat dry. In
a small bowl, mix salad oil,
fennel seeds, sherry, salt, minced
sage and parsley in a small bowl.
Brush fish both inside and
outside with the oil mixture.
Loosely wrap fish tail in foil.
Place butter, orange juice and
sugar in a small metal saucepan
with a metal handle. Place fish in
a well-oiled grilling basket or on
preheated, well-oiled grill (or
under the broiler), cover grill if
possible. Grill over medium-
high heat, basting with the
orange butter which has been
warming on the grill as the fish
cooks. Cook about 5-6 minutes
per side or until fish is nicely
browned, blistered and flakes
when fork-tested. When
completely cooked, fish should
be opaque, texture firm, moist
and flake into chunks when fork
tested. Serve on a warm platter;
pour remaining orange butter
over the fish and garnish with
sage and parsley sprigs.
Serves 4.

Caribbean-Style Red Snapper with Mango Salsa

Ingredients:

1 lb (454 g) **Red Snapper** fillets
1 Tbsp (15 ml) **lime juice**
1 Tbsp (15 ml) **water**
1 tsp (5 ml) **paprika**
½ tsp (2 ml) **salt** or to taste
¼ tsp (1 ml) ground **ginger**
¼ tsp (1 ml) ground **allspice**
¼ tsp (1 ml) **pepper**
1 recipe Mango **Salsa** (recipe follows)
1 medium **lime** (optional)
Parsley OR **cilantro** sprigs (optional)

Method:

Rinse fish under cold running water and pat dry. Cut into 4 serving size pieces. Mix lime juice and water together and brush on each fillet. Combine paprika, salt, ginger, allspice and pepper in a small bowl and rub gently onto fish. Arrange in a well greased, shallow baking dish. Bake in a 425°F (220°C) oven, uncovered, for 4-6 minutes for each ½ inch (1.5 cm) thickness of fish. When cooked the fish should be opaque and flake when fork-tested. Brush with pan juices and arrange on a serving platter. Garnish with lime wedges and parsley or cilantro sprigs. Serve with Mango Salsa.

Mango Salsa

Ingredients:

1 **mango**, peeled, seeded and chopped about 1 ½ cups (375 ml)
1 medium red sweet **pepper**, seeded and finely chopped
¼ cup (60 ml) green **onions**, thinly sliced
1 hot green chili **pepper**, seeded and finely chopped (wear rubber gloves while chopping)
½ tsp (2 ml) **lime** peel, finely shredded
3 Tbsp (45 ml) **olive oil**
2 Tbsp (30 ml) **lime juice**
1 Tbsp (15 ml) **vinegar**
¼ tsp (1 ml) **salt**
¼ tsp (1 ml) **pepper**

Method:

In a glass bowl, mix all ingredients together, cover and let stand in refrigerator for at least 1 hour to blend flavors. Makes 2 cups.

Bull Harbor Pan-Fried Snapper

Ingredients:
  1 cup (250 ml) Westcoaster Shakin' Bake **coating mix**, see recipe page 114
  ½ inch (1 cm) (approximately) vegetable **oil** for fry pan
  1 ½ lbs (750 g) **Snapper** fillets
  Tartar sauce
  1 **lemon**, sliced

Method:
  Moisten fish slightly with water and place into a plastic bag that contains the coating mix. Place a few pieces of fish in the bag and shake to coat fish evenly. Let fish stand several minutes until coating seems moist. Heat oil in a large cast iron fry pan, fry fillets for 3-4 minutes per side or until golden brown and fish flakes when fork-tested. Do not over-crowd pan, add more oil if necessary. Drain fish on paper towels and keep warm until all are ready to serve. Serve with Tartar Sauce, see recipe on page 12. Serves 4.

Arch Cape Baked Snapper

Ingredients:
  2 lbs (1 kg) **Snapper** fillets, cut into serving-size pieces
  ¼ cup (60 ml) **oil**
  2 Tbsp (30 ml) **orange juice**
  2 tsp (10 ml) **orange rind**, grated
  2 Tbsp (30 ml) **lemon juice**
  ½ tsp (2 ml) **salt**
  Dash **nutmeg**
  Dash **pepper**

Method:
  Rinse fish under cold running water. Pat dry. Place fish in a single layer in a well greased baking dish. In a small bowl, combine oil, orange juice, rind, lemon juice, salt, nutmeg and pepper; pour over fish. Bake in a 350°F (180°C) oven for about 20-25 minutes or until fish is opaque and easily flakes when fork-tested.

Sole

This section on the cooking of sole, also known as flatfish, could easily be a section on cooking flounder. The two fish are generally interchangeable in the following recipes. The West Coast is abundant with these mild-tasting fish. Sole have a lean white or off-white flesh which is fine textured. The skin is also edible but scrape off the scales before cooking.

How do you tell when sole is cooked: it should be opaque and should also flake into chunks when fork-tested in the thickest portion of the fish, yet still be moist looking. If sole is over-cooked, it will be dry and fall apart. Bake sole according to recipes but just before allotted time, check by the fork-testing method.

Things you won't hear a fisherman say...

Duct tape won't fix that.

I've never gotten the hang of sharpening a knife.

My truck won't go through that.

Let's go shopping, fishing can wait.

I feel pretty guilty not washing those breakfast dishes before coming out here to fish!

No, my fish wasn't that big.

I think these electronic fish finders should be banned.

We gotta throw this fish back, I don't think it will fit in the frying pan.

Microwaved Sole Rolls
with Asparagus

Ingredients:

¾ lb (350 g) fresh
asparagus
2 Tbsp (30 ml) **water**
3 Tbsp (45 ml) plain, low-
fat **yogurt**
1 Tbsp (15 ml) **corn starch**
¼ tsp (1 ml) dried whole
tarragon
1 Tbsp (15 ml) reduced-
calorie **mayonnaise**
½ tsp (2 ml) prepared
mustard
4 **sole** fillets,
(4 oz / 115 g ea)
2 Tbsp (30 ml) seasoned
dried **bread crumbs**

Method:

Prepare asparagus by
snapping off tough ends,
removing scales with a potato
peeler and rinsing under cold
running water. Place asparagus
in a 11 inch x 7 inch x 2 inch
(28 x 17 x 5 cm) baking dish
with trimmed ends toward the
outside of the dish. Add water,
cover with heavy-duty plastic
wrap and vent. Microwave on
HIGH 2 minutes or until
tender-crisp. Drain. Divide into
4 portions and set aside. In a
small bowl, combine yogurt
and corn starch; stir well. To
yogurt mixture add tarragon,
mayonnaise and mustard
stirring well. Over each fillet
spread 1 tsp (5 ml) of the yogurt
mixture. Divide asparagus into
4 bundles. Lay one bundle on
each fillet. Roll up as for a jelly
roll. Arrange, seam side down,
in a baking dish with asparagus
tips toward the inside of the
dish. Pour remaining yogurt
mixture over the rolls and
sprinkle with bread crumbs.
Cover with heavy-duty plastic
wrap, vent and cook on HIGH
for 5-6 minutes, or until fish is
opaque and flakes when fork-
tested. Rotate dish half way
through if your microwave
doesn't have a turn table. Let
stand covered for 3 minutes.

Poached Tillamook Stuffed Sole

Ingredients:
- 6 **sole** fillets (6" / 15 cm) long
- **Salt** and **pepper** to taste
- ¼ tsp (1 ml) **basil**
- 3 small firm **tomatoes**, cut in half horizontally
- 3 cups (750 ml) **salted water** (add **salt** according to taste)
- 1 **bay leaf**

Method:

Rinse fillets and pat dry. Season fish with salt, pepper and basil. Fold each fillet in half lengthwise and wrap around tomato half. Secure each roll with wooden toothpicks. Pour water in a skillet, add bay leaf and bring to simmer. Gently place rolls into water. Cover skillet and gently poach for 5-6 minutes, fish should be opaque and flake when fork-tested. Serve with a Cucumber Sauce, see recipe on page 47. Serves 6.

Baked Sole with Cream Sauce

Ingredients:
- 2 lbs (1 kg) **sole** fillets
- **Salt** and **pepper** to taste
- ½ cup (125 ml) **sour cream** OR **yogurt**
- 3 Tbsp (45 ml) **mayonnaise** OR **salad dressing**
- 1 ½ tsp (7 ml) **lemon juice**
- ½ cup (125 ml) **cucumber**, peeled and seeded
- ¼ tsp (1 ml) dried **dill**
- ½ tsp (2 ml) **lemon rind**, grated
- 1 green **onion**, chopped
- 1 Tbsp (15 ml) **parsley**, chopped

Method:

Rinse fillets and pat dry. Season fish with salt and pepper. Place fillets in a lightly greased oblong baking dish. Combine remaining ingredients in a small bowl and spread evenly over fillets. Preheat oven to 400°F (200°C) and bake for approximately 10-12 minutes or until fish is opaque and flakes when tested with a fork.

Linguine with Sole Sauce

Ingredients:
  1 lb (454 g) **linguine**
  1 Tbsp (15 ml) vegetable
  oil
  ¼ cup (60 ml) green
  onions, sliced
  ½ cup (125 ml)
  mushrooms, sliced
  1 small red **pepper**,
  slivered
  1 cup (250 ml) chicken
  broth
  12 oz (375 g) **sole** fillet, cut
  into 1 inch (2.5 cm)
  cubes
  ¾ cup (175 ml) **milk**
  1 Tbsp (15 ml) **corn starch**
  ½ tsp (2 ml) **salt** or to taste
  ¼ tsp (1 ml) dried **thyme**
  ¼ tsp (1 ml) **celery** seed
  ⅛ tsp (.5 ml) **pepper**
  ¼ cup (60 ml) **parsley**,
  finely chopped

Method:
  Cook linguine per package
directions. Drain. While pasta
is cooking, heat oil in a fry pan
over medium heat. Sauté
green onions, mushrooms and
red pepper for 1 minute. Stir
in broth. Bring to a boil, add
fish, cover and simmer for
about 6 minutes or until fish is
opaque and flakes when fork-
tested. In a small bowl
combine milk with corn starch,
salt, thyme, celery seed and
pepper. Stir into fish in fry
pan. Cook and stir over
medium-high heat until
mixture boils and thickens.
Serve hot fish sauce over pasta
and top with parsley. Serves 4.

*Salmon or other fatty fish
contain omega-3 fats which may
reduce the risk of heart attack.*

Sole with Almonds

Ingredients:
- 2 lbs (1 kg) **sole** fillets
- ½ cup (125 ml) **flour**
- 1 tsp (5 ml) **salt**
- ¼ tsp (1 ml) **pepper**
- 1 tsp (5 ml) **paprika**
- 3 Tbsp (45 ml) **butter**
- 3 Tbsp (45 ml) slivered blanched **almonds**
- 3 Tbsp (45 ml) **lemon juice**
- 1 tsp (5 ml) **lemon rind**, grated
- 3 Tbsp (45 ml) **chives**, chopped
- ⅓ cup (80 ml) cooking **oil**

Method:

Cut fish into serving-size pieces. In a medium-size flat dish, combine flour, salt, pepper and paprika. Coat fish on both sides with flour mixture and set aside. In a small skillet heat butter. Add almonds and cook while stirring until almonds are golden brown. Stir in lemon juice, rind and chives and keep warm. In a large heavy skillet over medium high, heat oil and fry fish quickly on both sides until golden brown and fish flakes when fork-tested, about 4-5 minutes per side. Lift cooked sole onto serving platter and pour almond sauce over the top. Serve while hot and crispy. Serves 6.

Inlet Sole in Spinach Sauce

Ingredients:

2 lbs (1 kg) **sole** fillets
Salt and **pepper** to taste
1 pkg. (12 oz/340 g)
   frozen **spinach**, chopped
1 tsp (5 ml) **onion**, finely
   chopped
1 Tbsp (15 ml) **butter**
½ tsp (2 ml) **salt** or to taste
Dash **pepper**
¼ cup (60 ml) **butter**
¼ cup (60 ml) **flour**
2 cups (500 ml) **milk**
1 tsp (5 ml) **salt**
⅛ tsp (.5 ml) **pepper**
¼ tsp (1 ml) dry **mustard**
½ cup (125 ml) sharp
   Cheddar **cheese**, grated

Method:

Preheat oven to 425°F
(220°C). Butter a
12 inch x 7 inch x 1 ½ inch
(28 x 17 x 3.7 cm) baking dish.
Lay largest of fillets on the
bottom of dish and season with
salt and pepper. Heat spinach
by adding a little water to pan,
cover and heat until spinach
can just be broken apart. Drain.
To the spinach add onion,
1 Tbsp (15 ml) butter, ½ tsp
(2 ml) salt and a dash of pepper.
Spoon this mixture over fillets
in baking dish and top with
remaining fish. In a medium-
size saucepan heat ¼ cup
(60 ml) butter. Sprinkle the
flour into butter, stirring to
blend. Cook 2-3 minutes.
Remove from heat, add milk,
stirring until well blended. Add
1 tsp (5 ml) salt, ⅛ tsp (.5 ml)
pepper and mustard. Return to
heat and cook, stirring
constantly, until thickened,
boiling and smooth. Pour this
mixture over the fish and
sprinkle with cheese. Bake for
20 minutes or until fish is
opaque and flakes when fork-
tested. Serves 4-6.

Oven Fried Sole

Ingredients:
- 2 lbs (1 kg) fresh or frozen **sole** OR **flounder** fillets
- ½ cup (125 ml) **buttermilk**
- 2 tsp (10 ml) **salt**
- ⅛ tsp (.5 ml) **pepper**
- ½ tsp (2 ml) dried leaf **thyme**, crumbled
- 1 cup (250 ml) **bread crumbs**, fine dry
- 2 Tbsp (30 ml) **parsley**, finely chopped
- 2 Tbsp (30 ml) cooking **oil**

Method:
If fish is frozen, thaw until fillets can be separated easily. Preheat oven to 425°F (220°C). Rinse fish under running water and pat dry. Cut into serving size pieces. In a medium-size bowl, combine buttermilk, salt, pepper and thyme. In a second bowl combine bread crumbs and parsley. Dip fish in buttermilk mixture then into crumbs, coating evenly. Coat a 13" x 9" x 2" (34 x 22 x 5 cm) baking dish with non-stick cooking spray and lay fish in a single layer in the bottom. Drizzle with cooking oil. Bake 10 minutes per inch of thickness, about 12-15 minutes. Fish should be opaque and flake when fork tested . Do not turn fish over. Serve while hot and crispy with Tartar Sauce, see recipe on page 12. Serves 6.

Soups and Stews

Gray skies threatening rain, cedar tops swaying with a southwester and you'd rather sit in front of a warm fire than worry about preparing a big dinner. Friends coming from out-of-town and you really want to do something memorable? Why not prepare a large pot of seafood chowder, soup or stew?

Bread, butter and a steaming bowl of chowder, you have just created a simple west coast tradition your friends are sure to talk about.

Fish Stock

Ingredients:

4 lbs (2 kg) **fish heads**,
bones and **trimmings** of
any non-oily **white fish**
2 Tbsp (30 ml) **butter** OR
margarine
1 large **onion**, diced
2 **carrots**, diced
2 stalks **celery**, diced
8 cups (2 l) cold **water**
2 **peppercorns**
1 **clove**
1 **bay leaf**
Sprig of **parsley**

Method:

Remove gills from fish. Clean
blood from fish heads and
wash under cold running
water. In a large stock pot over
medium heat, melt butter, add
onions, carrots and celery, cook
until tender approximately 10
minutes. Add fish heads, bones
and cold water making sure
there is enough to cover
ingredients by at least one inch
(2.5 cm). Tie seasonings in a
cheese cloth bag. Add to stock
pot. Increase heat to medium
high, bring to a boil and cook
for 5 minutes, skimming off any
scum. Reduce to low, simmer
for 45 minutes, uncovered.
Remove and strain stock
through several thicknesses of
cheesecloth. Refrigerate
immediately. Makes about
1 ½ qt (1 ½ l). Use as all or part
of the liquid in chowders,
soups, or bisques. You can
freeze this stock for use later.

Chinese Egg Flower Shrimp Soup

Ingredients:

1 lb (454 g) medium-size fresh **shrimp**, peeled and deveined

Fresh **ginger**, peeled, cut into 8 quarter-size slices

5 cups (1.25 l) low-salt chicken **broth**

2 tsp (10 ml) low-**salt soy sauce**

1 cup (250 ml) frozen **peas**, thawed

½ cup (125 ml) green **onions**, thinly sliced

2 large **eggs**, lightly beaten

Salt and **pepper** to taste

Method:

Rinse shrimp and pat dry. With back of knife, pound ginger so juices can permeate soup. In a medium-size saucepan, combine ginger, broth and soy sauce. Cover and bring to a boil; reduce heat and simmer for 5 minutes. Remove and discard ginger. Return to boiling; add shrimp, peas, and green onions. Drizzle eggs slowly into boiling soup, stir with a knife or a chopstick, cover and immediately remove pot from heat. Let stand until shrimp is white in center, about 2-3 minutes, stir soup so eggs break up, add salt and pepper. Serve hot with fried or baked wanton wrappers on the side. Serves 4-6.

The old custom is that Christmas celebrations begin on Christmas Eve with a Thanksgiving meal of salt fish followed by sweet raisin bread called "Christmas Fruit Loaf." Fishing was the means of livelihood and so fish had its place in thanksgiving before the day of feasting.

BYOF* Cioppino (Soup) Party

Bring Your Own Fish

Cioppino Base

Ingredients:
- ¼ cup (60 ml) **olive oil**
- 2 **onions**, chopped
- 3 ribs (1 ½ cups/375 ml) **celery**, chopped
- 6-8 **cloves garlic**, minced
- 3 **bay leaves**
- 1 tsp (5 ml) each: dried **basil**, **oregano**, **thyme**, marjoram
- ¼ tsp (1 ml) black **pepper**
- ¼ tsp (1 ml) dried red **pepper** flakes
- 2 cans (28 oz/796 ml ea) diced **tomatoes** in juice, undrained
- 1 tsp (5 ml) **sugar**
- 2 cans (6 oz/170 ml ea) **tomato paste**
- 1 can (1 qt/1 l approx.) **clam juice** OR **fish stock**
- 3 cups (750 ml) dry white **wine**
- 1 can (14 ½ oz/425 ml) chicken **broth**
- 4 sprigs fresh **parsley**
- 1 tsp (5 ml) **salt** or to taste

Mixed Seafood

Ingredients:
- 2 whole **crabs** (still in shell but cleaned)
- 1 lb (454 g) each: **snapper**, **salmon, halibut**; cut in 2 inch (5 cm) pieces
- 1 lb (454 g) large fresh **shrimp**, peeled
- 1 ½ lbs (750 g) **clams**, scrubbed

Method:

In fry pan, heat oil, sauté onion, celery and garlic. Stir in seasonings. In large pot, combine sautéed onion mixture, tomatoes, sugar, tomato paste, clam juice, wine, chicken broth, parsley and salt. Bring to boil, lower heat and cook for 30 minutes, stir often. Refrigerate overnight. Remove bay leaves and parsley. About 30 minutes before you want to eat, bring base to boil. Add crab, snapper, salmon and halibut. Simmer until fish is cooked. Fish should be opaque and flake when fork-tested, about 5-8 minutes. Crabs should turn a bright pinkish-orange color. Add shrimp and clams. Cook until shrimp turns white, about 3 minutes and clams open, about 6 minutes. Discard any clams that do not open. Serves 12-16.

New England Clam Chowder

Ingredients:
3 large **potatoes**, cubed
2 **carrots**, sliced
4 strips **bacon**, diced
2 small **onions**, chopped
2 stocks of **celery**, sliced
¼ cup (60 ml) **margarine**
¼ cup (60 ml) **flour**
2 cups (500 ml) **milk**
1 cup (250 ml) **water**
1 can (5 oz / 142 ml) whole baby **clams**, minced, reserve liquid
1 can (13.5 oz / 385 ml) **evaporated canned milk**
Salt to taste
½ tsp (2 ml) **pepper**
Parsley, snipped

Method:
In a separate pot boil potatoes and carrots adding only enough water to cover. Cook until tender, drain, reserve water and set aside. In a large heavy stock pot, fry bacon pieces, onion and celery until bacon is crisp and vegetables golden. In bacon drippings, melt margarine, mix in flour until a smooth paste is formed and flour is absorbed. Cook for 3 minutes over low heat until very slightly browned. Slowly add milk and water, stirring constantly until boiling, smooth and thickened. Carefully mix in cooked potatoes, carrots and reserved water from vegetables. Add clams, juice and the evaporated canned milk. Let simmer until hot but do not boil. Add salt and pepper, top with parsley. Serves 4.

Manhattan Clam Chowder

Ingredients:
8 strips of **bacon**
¼ cup (60 ml) **margarine**
½ cup (125 ml) **celery**, chopped
1 large **onion**, chopped
3 **cloves garlic**, minced
1 medium-size green **pepper**, chopped
¼ cup (60 ml) **flour**
2 cups (500 ml) **water**
6 cups (1.5 l) soup **stock**
4 large **potatoes**, cubed
2 large **carrots**, sliced
½ tsp (2 ml) **savory**
½ tsp (2 ml) **thyme**
Salt and **pepper** to taste
1 can (28 oz/796 ml) **tomatoes**, diced, reserve juice
2 cans (5 oz/142 g) baby **clams**, diced, reserve juice

Method:
In a large heavy stock pot, fry bacon until crisp. Remove bacon from pot, cool, crumble. Add margarine to bacon drippings. Add celery, onion, garlic and green pepper, saute until tender. Stir in flour until absorbed. Stir and cook 2-3 minutes until lightly browned. Slowly stir in water and soup stock until smooth, thick and boiling. Stir in bacon, remainder of vegetables and seasonings according to taste. Cook until vegetables are tender. Add canned tomatoes and simmer for 5 minutes. Add clams with juice, heat through but do not boil. Adjust seasonings. Serve immediately. Serves 8.

Garth's Christmas Chowder

Contributed by Holly Cameron, Tofino, B.C., Canada

Ingredients:

1 cup (250 ml) **butter**
1 small **onion**, chopped
½ cup (125 ml) **flour**
4 qt (4 l) **milk**
3 good-sized **potatoes**, cubed
6 medium **carrots**, chopped
4 ribs **celery**, sliced
3 lbs (1.5 kg) fresh **shrimp**, peeled and deveined, if desired OR octopus OR squid
2 lbs (1 kg) white fish (**cod**, **halibut** OR **black cod**), cubed
3 cans (8 oz / 227 ml ea) **clams**

Method:

In a large heavy soup pot, melt butter and sauté onions. Slowly stir in flour, cook for 3 minutes. Slowly stir in milk until it is smooth and thick. Add potatoes. Heat to just below boiling. Do not boil milk! Add carrots and celery. When vegetables are crisp, (still a little crunchy) add fish and shrimp. Cook until fish is done. Fish should flake easily when fork-tested, and is opaque, about 5-6 minutes. Shrimp is cooked when white, about 2-3 minutes). Add canned clams and heat through. Serve hot. One bowl is never enough!

Cape Elizabeth Crab Soup

Ingredients:

1 ½ Tbsp (22 ml) **butter**
1 ½ Tbsp (22 ml) **flour**
1 tsp (5 ml) dry **mustard**
¼ tsp (1 ml) **pepper**
½ tsp (2 ml) **celery salt**
½ tsp (2 ml) **salt**
1 Tbsp (15 ml **Worcestershire sauce**
3 cups (750 ml) hot **milk**
1 cup (250 ml) **crab meat**, cooked

Method:

In a deep saucepan melt butter. Add flour, mustard, pepper, celery salt, salt and Worcestershire. Stir constantly until flour is absorbed. Cook for 3 minutes. Add hot milk to flour mixture, stirring until smooth, thick and hot, but do not boil. Add crab meat, heat through. Serve with additional Worcestershire or Tabasco sauce. Serves 4.

Shrimp Gumbo

Ingredients:
- 1 large **onion**
- 2 ribs **celery**
- 1 **clove garlic**, minced
- 1 whole **chicken** (3 lbs/1.5 kg)
- 8 cups (2 l) **water**
- 1 ½ tsp (7 ml) **salt**, divided
- ½ red or green **pepper**
- ½ cup (125 ml) **oil**
- 4 oz (115 g) **ham** steak cut into ½ inch (1.5 cm) pieces
- ½ cup (125 ml) **flour**
- ¾ tsp (4 ml) dried **thyme**
- ¾ tsp (4 ml) dried **oregano**
- ¼ tsp (1 ml) cayenne **pepper**
- ¼ tsp (1 ml) black **pepper**
- 1 (9 oz/255 g) frozen **broccoli**, thawed
- ½ lb (250 g) medium fresh **shrimp**, peeled, deveined
- 8 cups (2 l) hot cooked, long-grain **rice**

Method:

One day before serving, make stock by placing half of the onion, half of the celery, and minced garlic clove in a large pot with chicken and water, add ¾ tsp (4 ml) salt. Bring to boil, cover and simmer until chicken meat falls off the bones. About 2 hours. Remove chicken, strain stock and discard vegetables. When chicken is cool, discard skin, pull meat from bones and cut into small pieces. While stock cooks, chop remaining onion, celery and bell pepper. Heat oil in a large, heavy pot, until very hot. Add ham, stirring constantly, until browned. Remove ham and set aside. Stir flour into oil and cook, stirring constantly with wooden spoon, until medium-brown. About 10 minutes. Add remaining salt, vegetables, thyme, oregano, cayenne and black pepper. Cook, stirring constantly until flour mixture turns dark brown, about 10 minutes. Take care not to burn. Stir in 4 cups of chicken stock. Bring to boil, reduce heat and stir until smooth and thick. Cook until vegetables are tender. Add chicken and ham, stir. Remove from heat and let cool. Cover and refrigerate overnight.

Just before serving:

In a heavy pot over medium-high heat, bring gumbo to a boil, stirring occasionally. Add broccoli and shrimp, and cook until shrimp is white, about 2-3 minutes. Serve over rice. Serves 8. Can easily be doubled to serve 16.

Crab Bisque

Ingredients:

6 Tbsp (90 ml) **butter**, divided

4 Tbsp (60 ml) **onion**, chopped

4 Tbsp (60 ml) green **pepper**, chopped

1 **scallion** OR **green onion**, coarsely chopped

2 Tbsp (30 ml) **parsley**, chopped

1 cup (250 ml) **mushrooms**, sliced

2 Tbsp (30 ml) **flour**

1 ½ cup (375 ml) **milk**

Salt and **pepper** to taste

Dash **paprika**

Dash red **pepper sauce**

1 cup (250 ml) **cream**

2 pkgs (6 oz / 170 g ea) frozen **crabmeat***, thawed

3 Tbsp (45 ml) dry **Sherry**

Method:

In a small fry pan melt 4 Tbsp (60 ml) butter and sauté onion, green pepper, scallion, parsley and mushrooms until soft, set aside. Heat remaining butter in large, heavy saucepan. Remove from heat. Stir in flour. Return to heat and slowly add milk, stirring constantly until thick and smooth. Stir in salt, pepper, paprika and pepper sauce. Stir in sautéed vegetables and cream. Add crab and Sherry, heat through. Simmer uncovered for 5 minutes. Do not boil.

*Lobster or shrimp can be substituted.

Fish Mulligan

Contributed by Hilda Brown, Victoria, B.C., Canada

Ingredients:

2 Tbsp (30 ml) **oil**

1 lb (454 g) any firm, **lean fish**, cut into bite-size pieces

2 large **onions**, chopped

¼ cup (60 ml) green **peppers**, diced

1 stock of **celery** with top, chopped

4 cups (1 l) fish OR chicken **stock**

4 large **potatoes**, cubed

2 **carrots**, sliced

1 can (28 oz / 796 ml) **tomatoes**

1 cup (250 ml) cooked **rice**

¼ tsp (1 ml) powdered **thyme**

2 Tbsp (30 ml) **parsley**, minced

Salt and **pepper** to taste

Method:

In a large heavy stock pot, add oil and saute fish, onions, green pepper and celery until lightly browned. Remove fish and set aside. Stir in stock, potatoes, carrots and cook until tender crisp. Add tomatoes and rice, simmer 5 minutes. Add fish. Cook for a few minutes until fish easily flakes when fork-tested and heated through. Season with thyme, parsley, salt and pepper. Serve.

Moclips Seafood Stew

Ingredients:

2 Tbsp (30 ml) **olive oil**

3 small **leeks**, white parts only, sliced in ½ inch (1.5 cm) diagonal pieces, rinsed

2 **garlic cloves**, minced

⅓ cup (80 ml) fresh **dill**, chopped, well packed

4 cups (1 l) vegetable **stock**

½ cup (125 ml) dry white **wine**

1 Tbsp (15 ml) **lemon juice**

Salt and white **pepper** to taste

1 lb (454 g) firm-fleshed **white fish** (such as cod or red snapper)

1 lb (454 g) fresh **shrimp**, peeled and deveined

⅓ cup (80 ml) **flour**

1 Tbsp (15 ml) **butter**, room temperature

Method:

In a large stock pot, heat oil over medium-low heat. Add leeks, garlic and dill. Cook until slightly softened, stirring often. Stir in remaining ingredients, except flour, butter and seafood. Cover, bring to a gentle boil then reduce heat and simmer for 15 minutes. In a small bowl combine flour and butter, blend in ½ cup (125 ml) pot juices. Slowly stir back into stew. Bring to a boil and cook until smooth and thick. Cut fish into large bite-size pieces, stir into sauce, cover and cook for 2 minutes. Add shrimp and continue cooking until fish are opaque and flake easily when fork-tested and shrimp are white, about 3 more minutes. Do not overcook seafood. Serve immediately.

Tuna

What recipe book would be complete without recipes for the versatile tuna? Bluefin, Yellowfin, Skipjack, and Bigeye are names of tuna found in Northwest waters. Of the four named above, the Skipjack is probably the most widely caught.

Tuna meat has a taste all its own and is firm and compact. The best part of the fish is the belly, prized for steaks and fillets. The skin on tuna is not edible. Also, the dark areas on the flesh of tuna have a bitter taste and most people trim this part off. Tuna is excellent raw otherwise barbecued and grilled tuna steaks are delicious. Try pan-fried tuna steaks. Of course, for those of us who don't catch our own fish, tuna is available in all forms from frozen to canned.

Cajun Barbecued Tuna

Ingredients:
- ½ cup (125 ml) **Cajun Marinade**, see recipe on page 17
- 4 **tuna** steaks, 7 oz ea (200 g ea), 1 inch (2.5 cm) thick

Method:
Pour marinade evenly over steaks, let stand at least 30 minutes in the refrigerator, covered, turning several times. Drain steaks, cook on an open well-oiled grill over medium hot heat. Baste fish and turn once while cooking. Grill about 1 minute per side for medium rare, 2-3 minutes per side for rare or about 4-6 minutes per side for medium. Fish is cooked when opaque and fish flakes when fork-tested.

Pan-fried Tuna Steaks

Ingredients:
- 2 Tbsp (30 ml) Mediterranean Spice **Rub**, see recipe on page 17
- ¼ cup (60 ml) **olive oil**
- 1 Tbsp (30 ml) **olive oil**
- 4 **tuna** steaks, 5 oz ea (200 g ea), ½ inch (1 cm) thick

Method:
In a small glass bowl, combine rub with ¼ cup (60 ml) olive oil. In a shallow glass dish large enough to hold tuna, pour marinade in, coat tuna on both sides. Cover and refrigerate for at least 1 hour, turning occasionally. In a large cast iron fry pan over high heat, add remaining oil, fry tuna steaks until golden brown on the outside, but cooked to desired doneness on the inside. 1 minute per side for medium rare, 2-3 minutes per side for rare or about 4-6 minutes per side for medium. Fish is cooked when opaque and fish flakes when fork-tested.

Italian-style Tuna Strips

Ingredients:
½ tsp (2 ml) **basil**
½ tsp (2 ml) **oregano**
½ tsp (2 ml) dried **mint**,
   crushed fine
Salt and **pepper** to taste
3 Tbsp (45 ml) **olive oil**,
   divided
3 **cloves** of **garlic**, minced
1 large sweet **onion**, sliced
   in rings
1 large green **pepper**,
   chopped
2 large **tomatoes**, cored
   and chopped
1 ½ lbs (800 g) **tuna** fillets,
   cut into 1 inch (2.5 cm)
   wide strips

Method:
In a small dish combine seasonings, set aside. In a large heavy skillet, over medium heat, add 1 Tbsp (15 ml) olive oil and garlic, onion, green pepper and tomatoes. Let simmer for 5-10 minutes. Remove to warm oven. If necessary, clean skillet with paper towel, and add the remaining olive oil, increase heat to high. Sprinkle the seasonings over the tuna strips and gently rub in with your fingers. In hot skillet, quickly sear tuna strips on both sides. Do not over-crowd pan. Add more oil if necessary for additional batches. Cook just 3-4 minutes, turning once or until golden brown and fish flakes when fork-tested or, to desired doneness. Serve with simmered vegetables and rice.

Sechelt Tuna Casserole

Ingredients:
Butter
12 slices **bread**
2 cans (7 oz / 199 ml ea)
  water-packed **tuna**,
  drained and flaked
1 cup (250 ml) **celery**,
  chopped
½ cup (125 ml) **onion**,
  thinly sliced
2 cups (500 ml) **milk**
1 cup (250 ml) **mayonnaise**
4 **eggs**, slightly beaten
1 can (10 oz / 284 g) Cream
  of mushroom **soup**
⅛ tsp (.5 ml) **dill** OR
  thyme (optional)
1 cup (250 ml) **potato
  chips** OR **corn flakes**,
  slightly crushed
3 slices processed **cheese**

Method:
Butter one side of each slice of bread and arrange six of the slices, butter side down, in the bottom of a 9 inch x 13 inch (23 x 34 cm) baking pan. Arrange tuna over the bread slices. Top with the celery and half of the onion. Cover with remaining bread slices, buttered side down. Set aside. Mix together the milk, mayonnaise, eggs, soup and dill or thyme. Pour over the bread in the pan. Top with the remaining onion. Cover and refrigerate over night. Uncover and bake at 350°F (180°C) for about 45-60 minutes. Sprinkle potato chips or corn flakes over the top. Arrange cheese slices in a pleasing pattern on top. Return to oven for 5-10 minutes, until cheese melts and top is lightly browned. Serves 8.

Salmon, herring and tuna are excellent sources of vitamin D. Vitamin D is important for healthy bones and may help prevent certain cancers.

Cape Scott Tuna Creole Dish

Ingredients:
 1 Tbsp (15 ml) **butter**
 1 medium **onion**, chopped
 ½ cup (125 ml) green
   pepper, chopped
 1 can (14 oz/398 ml)
   tomatoes, diced with juice
 ¼ tsp (1 ml) **thyme**
 ⅛ tsp (.5 ml) **cayenne** OR
   hot **pepper sauce**
 Salt and **pepper** to taste
 2 cans (7 oz/199 ml) **tuna**,
   undrained
 Hot cooked **rice**

Method:
 In cast iron fry pan melt
butter, saute onion and green
pepper until tender. Stir in
tomatoes and seasonings.
Simmer for 5 minutes stirring
occasionally. Flake tuna and
gently stir in. Cover and
simmer for 5 more minutes.
Serve over hot rice.

Creamed Tuna over Rice

Ingredients:
 2 Tbsp (30 ml) **butter**
 2 Tbsp (30 ml) **flour**
 1 cup (250 ml) hot **milk**
 ½ tsp (2 ml) **salt**
 1 **bay leaf**
 ¼ tsp (1 ml) **pepper**
 ½ tsp (2 ml) **onion**, grated
 2 cans (7 oz/199 ml ea)
   tuna OR any fish,
   drained
 ½ cup (125 ml) dry **bread**
   OR **cracker crumbs**,
   finely crushed
 Butter

Method:
 In top of double boiler melt
butter, add flour, stir until
blended. Gradually add hot
milk, stir until smooth. Cook
2-3 minutes. Add salt, bay leaf,
pepper, onion, stirring until
thick. Remove bay leaf. Lightly
grease baking dish, flake some
of the fish over bottom. Pour
half of the sauce over the fish
then layer fish and remainder of
sauce. Sprinkle with bread
crumbs and dot with butter.
Bake in a 350°F (180°C) oven
until lightly browned, about
15-20 minutes.

Tuna Potato Loaf

Ingredients:

2 cans (7 oz / 199 g ea) light
tuna, flaked and undrained
1 cup (250 ml) seasoned
mashed **potatoes**
½ cup (125 ml) **onion**, finely
minced
1 cup (250 ml) **celery**, finely
minced
½ tsp (2 ml) black **pepper**
½ tsp (2 ml) **thyme**
½ tsp (2 ml) **garlic salt**
1 cup (250 ml) **milk**
2 **eggs**, well beaten
2 cups (500 ml) cracker **crumbs**,
coarsely crushed

Method:

In a mixing bowl place
tuna, potatoes, onion, celery,
and seasonings. Stir in milk
and eggs. Fold in cracker
crumbs. Place mixture in a
greased loaf pan and bake in
a 350°F (180°C) oven for
1 hour or until center is set.
Cool for 10 minutes before
slicing. Serves 4- 6.

Tuna and Rice Patties

Ingredients:

1 can (7 oz / 199 ml) **tuna**,
drained
1 **egg**, beaten
½ cup (125 ml) cooked **rice**
½ cup (125 ml) **onion**,
chopped
¼ cup (60 ml) **Parmesan
cheese**, grated
¼ cup (60 ml) **buttermilk
baking mix** OR **pancake
mix**
¼ cup (60 ml) green **pepper**,
chopped
Salt and **pepper** to taste
Oil for frying

Method:

In a bowl, combine all
ingredients except oil until well
blended. Pour enough oil to
cover the bottom of a large
skillet and heat over medium
heat until hot. Drop a heaping
tablespoon of the tuna mixture
into the hot oil, flatten until
about ⅓ inch (1 cm) thick. Fry
3-4 minutes on each side or
until golden brown and firm.
Serve with lightly flavored
garlic bread and try it with
Cucumber Sauce, see recipe on
page 47.

Pat's Hardy Tuna Casserole

Ingredients:
3 cups/750 ml (6 oz/170 g)
uncooked **egg noodles**

1 can (7 oz/199 ml) **tuna**,
undrained

½ cup (125 ml) **celery**,
chopped

¼ cup (60 ml) green **onion**,
chopped

½ cup (125 ml) dairy **sour
cream**

2 tsp (10 ml) **mustard**

½ cup (125 ml) **mayonnaise**

½ tsp (2 ml) dried **thyme**
leaves

½ tsp (2 ml) **salt** or to taste

¼ tsp (1 ml) ground black
pepper

1 small **zucchini**, sliced

1 cup (250 ml) cheddar
cheese, grated

1 large **tomato**, chopped

Method:
Cook egg noodles according
to package directions and rinse
well in hot water, cool. Flake
tuna and stir into noodles with
celery and onions. In a separate
bowl blend sour cream,
mustard, mayonnaise and
seasonings, stir into tuna
mixture. Place half of the
mixture in a casserole dish
coated with non-stick cooking
spray, top with half of the
zucchini, repeat layers and top
with cheese. Bake in a 350°F
(180°C) oven for 30 minutes or
until golden and bubbly.
Spread tomato on top before
serving.

Puget Sound Tuna Pie

Ingredients:
- 1 Tbsp (15 ml) vegetable **oil**
- ½ cup (125 ml) **celery**, chopped
- 6 green **onions**, sliced
- 1 Tbsp (15 ml) **water**
- 3 Tbsp (45 ml) **flour**
- 2 cups (500 ml) vegetable, fish OR chicken **stock**
- ¼ tsp (1 ml) cayenne **pepper**
- White **pepper** to taste
- 1 cup (250 ml) frozen **peas**
- 1 can (12 oz/341 ml) **corn**, undrained
- ¼ cup (60 ml) **parsley**, chopped
- 2 cans (7 oz/199 g ea) **tuna**, drained and chunked
- 1 **egg white**, lightly beaten
- 3 cups (750 ml) seasoned mashed **potatoes**
- ½ cup (125 ml) **Parmesan cheese**, grated
- 1 Tbsp (15 ml) dry **bread crumbs**, crushed fine

Method:
Using a non-stick saucepan, heat oil over medium heat; add celery and onions, cook for 1 minute. Add water and reduce heat to medium-low; cook covered for 4 minutes or until onions are just tender. Slowly add flour while stirring until well blended. Gradually stir in stock, cayenne and white pepper. Cook, stirring constantly, until smooth and thickened. Add peas, corn and parsley, stir. Remove from heat. Stir in tuna to vegetables. Place mixture in a large casserole dish coated with non-stick cooking spray.

Mix lightly beaten egg white into mashed potatoes. Stir in cheese. Spread evenly over tuna mixture and sprinkle with bread crumbs. Bake in a 375°F (190°C) oven for 30-35 minutes or until potatoes are golden brown and tuna mixture is bubbly. Serves 6.

Rosalie's Tuna Noodle Casserole

Contributed by Rosalie Phillips, Victoria, B.C., Canada

Ingredients:
- 4 cups (1 l) cooked wide egg **noodles**
- 1 can (7 oz / 199 ml) **tuna**, drained, reserve liquid and flaked
- 1 tsp (5 ml) **parsley** finely chopped
- 1 tsp (5 ml) red **pepper**, finely chopped (optional)
- l tsp (5 ml) green **pepper**, finely chopped (optional)
- 1 tsp (5 ml) yellow **pepper**, finely chopped (optional)
- 2 **eggs**, hard-boiled, sliced (optional)
- 2 cups (500 ml) **cream sauce** (recipe follows)
- **Butter**
- ¼ cup (60 ml) dried **bread crumbs**, crushed
- ¼ cup (60 ml) **cheese**, grated (Cheddar is good)

Method:
In a bowl, toss together cooked noodles, tuna, parsley and peppers (if using) and eggs in a lightly greased casserole dish. Pour sauce mixed with reserved tuna juice over the noodle mixture. Dot with butter and sprinkle bread crumbs over the top followed by the grated cheese. Bake in a 350°F (180°C) oven until the cheese is golden brown, about 25-30 minutes.

Cream Sauce

Ingredients:
- 2 Tbsp (30 ml) **butter** OR **margarine**
- 2 Tbsp (30 ml) **flour**
- 1 cup (250 ml) **milk**, heated
- 1 cup (250 ml) **clam nectar** OR **chicken stock**, heated

Method:
Melt butter in the top of a double boiler. Add flour, stirring until all butter is absorbed, let cook 2-3 minutes. Gradually add heated milk and heated stock, stirring constantly until smooth and thickened. Makes 2 cups (500 ml).

Cracked Wheat Tuna Spread

Ingredients:
- 1 can (7 oz / 199 ml) **tuna**, drained
- ⅓ cup (80 ml) **celery**, diced
- ½ cup (125 ml) cooked **cracked wheat**
- 1 tsp (5 ml) **onion**, grated
- 1 cup (250 ml) **mayonnaise** OR **salad dressing**

Method:
In a bowl, mix all ingredients together until well blended. Spread on crackers as an appetizer or on bread for sandwiches.

Tuna in Shells

Ingredients:
- 1 pkg (12 oz / 375 g) jumbo shell macaroni
- 6 slices fresh white **bread**
- 1 can (7 oz / 199 ml) **tuna**, undrained
- 1 cup (250 ml) **celery**, minced
- ¼ cup (60 ml) **milk**
- ½ cup (125 ml) **walnuts**, finely chopped
- ¼ cup (60 ml) **onion**, minced
- 4 tsp (20 ml) **lemon juice**
- ¼ tsp (1 ml) coarsely ground **pepper** or to taste
- 1 Tbsp (15 ml) **brown sugar**
- 1 jar (32 oz / 910 ml)) **Marinara sauce** OR **Italian pasta sauce**

Method:
In a large saucepan, cook shells as directed on package. Drain and set aside. Preheat oven to 350°F (180°C). Cut bread slices into ¼ inch (1 cm) cubes. In a large bowl, mix bread cubes, tuna, celery, milk, walnuts, onion, lemon juice and pepper until well blended. Spoon mixture into shells. Blend brown sugar into sauce and spoon half into a 9 inch x 13 inch (23 x 34 cm) baking dish. Arrange shells in a single layer on top of sauce. Pour remaining sauce over the shells. Cover dish and bake for 40 minutes. Serves 8.

Crunchy Tuna Casserole

Ingredients:
- 1 can cream of mushroom **soup**
- ½ cup (125 ml) **milk**
- ½ cup (125 ml) **cheese**, grated
- 1 can (7 oz/199 ml) **tuna**, undrained and flaked
- ½ cup (125 ml) **onion**, chopped
- 2 **eggs**, hard-cooked, sliced
- 1 cup (250 ml) **peas**, cooked
- 1 cup (250 ml) chow mein **noodles**
- ⅓ cup (80 ml) **bread crumbs**, dried, crushed fine

Method:
Coat a 1 ½ qt. (1 ½ l) casserole with non-stick cooking spray. Blend soup, milk and cheese in casserole dish. Stir in tuna, onions, eggs and peas. Gently mix in noodles. Bake uncovered in a 350°F (180°C) oven for 20-25 minutes. Remove from oven, sprinkle crumbs on top. Bake an additional 5 minutes or until nicely browned. Serves 4.

Potato Topped Tuna Pie

Ingredients:
- 3 Tbsp (45 ml) **butter**
- 3 Tbsp (45 ml) **flour**
- 1 cup (250 ml) **milk**
- **Salt** to taste
- 1 can (7 oz/199 ml) **tuna**, undrained
- 1 cup (250 ml) cooked **peas**
- ½ cup (125 ml) **cheese**, grated
- 2 cups (500 ml) hot mashed **potatoes**

Method:
In fry pan over medium heat, melt butter, blend in flour and cook 2-3 minutes until absorbed. Gradually blend in milk, stirring until thick and smooth. Add salt. Mix in tuna and peas. Pour into a greased baking dish. Stir half the cheese into the potatoes. Spoon potato and cheese mixture over tuna in dish. Sprinkle with remaining cheese. Bake in a 350°F (180°C) oven for 15-20 minutes or until heated through.

Index

171

Salmon spend almost all of their life on a journey. Their journey is long and strange. It begins in a little freshwater pool. When the salmon are a few inches long, they leave their pool and swim into a stream. The stream turns into a river and the river takes them to the sea. Some salmon travel as much as two thousand miles before they reach the Pacific Ocean.

Salmon live about three years. When they reach maturity, they stop eating and turn toward the hardest part of their life journey. Their instincts guide the salmon back to the little pool where they were born.

It's believed that salmon have a tremendous sense of smell. They smell the water of the river that they originally journeyed down and begin fighting their way up streams, waterfalls and fast-moving currents. Once their nose guides them back to their little freshwater pool, they lay eggs and die!

The Westcoaster Apple Cookbook

The apple-of-every-apple-lover's-eye!

Apples are as much a part of our North American history as, well—apple pie! A collection of more than 200 tempting recipes. Apples can be served hundreds of interesting ways—from soup, salsa or catsup; for breakfast, lunch or dinner; to traditional or simply amazing desserts. You will find all your old favorites plus new recipes too!

The Westcoaster Family Cookbook

A Classic "Best Seller". Many readers report this cookbook as a family staple in their kitchen! A delightful collection of more than 300 tried and true family-favorite recipes. Completely updated and revised, new layout and color photos.

Maple Lane Publishing
1-800-270-6007
www.the-westcoaster.com